Coach Gibbs has always said that you win wi experience that running a race team can be d circumstances, but in recent years Joe Gibbs than most. Dave Alpern has been a steady in challenging times. *Taking the Lead* does a gre scenes and showing you how Dave and the n us continue to win at a high level. For as long as I've known him, Dave has shown endless energy doing his job at JGR. He is a respected executive within the NASCAR industry and is equally as dedicated to his family and his faith.

**KYLE BUSCH,** two-time NASCAR Cup Series champion and NASCAR's all-time wins leader

Without a doubt, Pern has led a lot of amazing things, and you are about to experience them in *Taking the Lead*. To me, though, I am most impressed and encouraged by who Dave *is*. It is his heart and character that is revealed throughout every page of this book. Dave is an incredible leader, father, "bro," friend, champion, Kingdom builder, and most importantly, a son of God. So enjoy every story, every leadership nugget, and most importantly, my servant-leading friend and his passion to strengthen others.

**JACK HOLLIS,** senior VP of automotive operations for Toyota Motor North America

I spent twelve years at Joe Gibbs Racing and got to know Dave really well. Even during the most challenging times, he kept a positive outlook. While he has learned a lot from Coach, Dave has always had an impressive work ethic and a keen understanding that the right way of doing things is the only way. He'll come out on top in a battle of wits, too. Dave's sense of humor puts everyone at ease. If you're looking for a leader, just look to Dave.

**TONY STEWART,** three-time NASCAR Cup Series champion and NASCAR Hall of Famer

Taking the Lead is an excellent story of leadership lessons learned while overcoming the personal challenges and self-doubt that all great leaders experience. But perhaps more importantly, it's a touching tribute to a best friend lost too early and to an amazing mentor in Coach Gibbs. Through a culture focused on people first, Joe Gibbs Racing has built a team that goes fast and delivers, operating with the fundamental belief that winning in life *is* winning the race.

**SHANNON LAPIERRE,** CCO of Stanley Black & Decker

I have had the privilege of knowing Dave Alpern since high school. Along with being a great father and husband, Dave embodies what it means to be a servant leader by leading with a meek strength that is rare in men. I have watched him serve with excellence throughout his many roles at JGR, and he has much wisdom to share with us through the principles he has learned on his journey from unpaid intern to president of JGR.

**TOBY MAC,** seven-time Grammy Award winner and multiplatinum recording artist

J.D.'s influence on this book, its author, and the DNA of Joe Gibbs Racing lives in these pages. I'm proud that Dave wrote this book so that others can see and ultimately learn from the culture Coach Gibbs and J.D. instilled in their top-flight organization. The style in which Dave offers real-life experiences followed by questions for the reader to reflect on is effective and thought-provoking.

**DENNY HAMLIN,** three-time Daytona 500 champion and driver of the #11 FedEx Toyota Camry for Joe Gibbs Racing

Dave Alpern has been a friend and mentor to me for more than twenty years, and his measured, graceful approach to leadership is rare and impactful. But nothing he has accomplished professionally has impacted me more deeply and personally than his wisdom. In a moment of great complexity and confusion for me as a father, Dave picked me up and walked me through his lifelong negotiation of Tourette's syndrome and the difficulty he faced in attempting to articulate that moment-by-moment negotiation to his own parents and friends. Seeing his success and relationship skills while managing Tourette's gave me tremendous hope.

**MARTY SMITH,** ESPN reporter/host and author of the *New York Times* bestseller *Never Settle: Sports, Family, and the American Soul*

Having been in relationship with Dave, Coach, J.D., and the JGR crew since the very beginning, I can say that alignment on the principles outlined by Dave in *Taking the Lead* are what brought us together, and those same principles have sustained our winning relationship for all these years. What a ride it has been!

**SCOTT MILLER,** CEO of Interstate Batteries

Dave has had the opportunity to work with leaders of successful corporations and with Hall of Fame coach Joe Gibbs during his career at Joe Gibbs Racing. This book does an excellent job distilling those experiences into practical advice to equip you to be more successful in your professional and personal life.

**T. MICHAEL GLENN,** retired executive vice president of FedEx

*Taking the Lead* is about a man's willingness to serve. Dave Alpern's humility, transparency, and perseverance are inspiring. But his abiding loyalty to those around him, especially to J.D. Gibbs, and his deep faith in Jesus Christ are at the foundation of his leadership and life story. In the end, we witness a leader who embodies the cultural values of Joe Gibbs Racing: honor God, put people before profits, and relentlessly pursue winning. It's like Dave is standing before us in the race of life and giving the command, "Ladies and gentlemen, start your engines!"

**NEWT CRENSHAW,** president and CEO of Young Life

I've known Dave since he and I both started working in NASCAR almost thirty years ago. I can tell you firsthand that Dave Alpern lives out the mission-driven life. After working for more than two decades alongside legendary Coach Joe Gibbs, one of the most focused and godly men on earth, Dave has a truly unique perspective on life as a leader, friend, father, and husband. I really admire Dave's steadfast commitment to his faith, his family, and his mission in life.

**MARCUS G. SMITH,** president and CEO of Speedway Motorsports

Dave's book is an inspiration for anyone looking for purpose or a North Star in their business or personal life. He reveals deeply personal stories on how he has learned to follow his heart and his faith and describes the great people he has learned those lessons from. Dave provides great insight on how to find motivation from the people around you, and his words on the importance of relationships and putting people first are a must-read for anyone looking to ensure their focus is on the things matter. I am proud to call Dave a friend and proud of him for sharing his wisdom and his faith so we can all learn from him.

**JILL GREGORY,** former NASCAR CMO and current executive vice president of Sonoma Raceway

It didn't take long for me to realize that Dave Alpern was not only a great person but was also going to grow into a great leader at JGR. We've spent a lot of time together over the years. Pern is a great friend, a great role model, and a man of God.

**BOBBY LABONTE,** Hall of Fame NASCAR driver

*Taking the Lead* is an engaging and inspiring celebration of life and faith by someone who knows he was blessed beyond measure, found his passion, did well, and did good. Whether you are a NASCAR fan or not, you'll find that Dave Alpern's story is an amazing saga of perseverance, creativity, dedication, and friendship.

**NICHOLAS DIDOW,** professor at the Kenan-Flagler Business School, University of North Carolina, Chapel Hill

Dave Alpern humbly and transparently shares his personal and professional journey and traces his rise from the "T-shirt guy" to the president of Joe Gibbs Racing. I loved hearing so many of Pern's familiar stories told within the context of rich business and life lessons.

**DAVID WILSON,** president of Toyota Racing Development (TRD)

Successful in family, faith, community, and career, Dave Alpern knows how to lead and the qualities it takes to be a great leader. And it starts with sharing, and that's exactly what he does here in this brilliant book.

**WILLIAM CLEMENTS,** general manager of Mars Properties and Family Brands

You should take the lead from Dave Alpern, a leader whose principles extend from his personal character to his business relationships. I can't think of a better person to learn from than Dave. With this book as a guide, each of us can be the Dave on our teams, leading them to even greater success.

**MONICA SKIPPER,** vice president of brand experience marketing at FedEx

This book is more than good; it's one of the most authentic and thought-provoking playbooks for winning in business and in life. Get ready to be challenged. Be prepared to see Dave's mastery in synthesizing our calling and maximizing our impact. If you ever wonder what it means to plan as if you'll live forever but *live* as if today is your last, this will get you going. This book will remind you why legacy matters and of the power of your yes.

**MANNY OHONME,** founder, president, and CEO of Samaritan's Feet International

I have lived a lot of life with my friend Dave Alpern, and I can honestly say few have combined business with keeping a nonstop Christlike posture the way Dave has. From stories about how to be a fountain and not a drain with your workmates, to how to care for what's most important in your life, to "traits of the greats," Dave shares his key life experiences to help you "take the lead" in your own life. Well done, Pernski!

**MARTY SNIDER,** NBC Sports

"Why me?" Who else but me! In *Taking the Lead*, Dave transparently walks us through a chapter of his life he never imagined and never wanted. In a moment of unexpected change, what does it take to rise to the occasion? Understanding the importance of relationships, and faith—real faith, not some folly or wild fairy tale, a faith Dave first witnessed in his dearest friend, a living example of Christ to him that he honors to this day. For each of us a moment comes when we, too, may be unexpectedly "taking the lead," and you, like Dave, can confidently conclude, "Who else but me?"

**BILLY MAULDIN,** president and senior chaplain of Motor Racing Outreach

Just as it is in our personal lives, faith is a critical element in business. Faith in your colleagues, your company, your mission, and most importantly, in a purpose far larger than your day-to-day work. Dave Alpern understands the relationship between faith and achieving true fulfillment in business and in life, and the rise and success of Joe Gibbs Racing is a testament to that achievement. In *Taking the Lead* Dave speaks to that connection and the ubiquitous role faith plays in leading a purpose-driven life. This book is a valuable read for anyone wanting to learn and improve.

**STEVE PHELPS,** president of NASCAR

WINNING BUSINESS
PRINCIPLES THAT FUEL
JOE GIBBS RACING

# DAVE ALPERN

with David Thomas

# TAKING THE LEAD

TYNDALE
MOMENTUM®

*The Tyndale nonfiction imprint*

*May the God of hope fill you with all joy*

*and peace as you trust in him,*

*so that you may overflow with hope*

*by the power of the Holy Spirit.*

ROMANS 15:13

Visit Tyndale online at tyndale.com.

Visit Tyndale Momentum online at tyndalemomentum.com.

*TYNDALE*, Tyndale's quill logo, *Tyndale Momentum*, and the Tyndale Momentum logo are registered trademarks of Tyndale House Ministries. Tyndale Momentum is the nonfiction imprint of Tyndale House Publishers, Carol Stream, Illinois.

*Taking the Lead: Winning Business Principles That Fuel Joe Gibbs Racing*

Designed by Ron C. Kaufmann

Published in association with the literary agency, WTA Media LLC, Franklin, TN.

For information about special discounts for bulk purchases, please contact Tyndale House Publishers at csresponse@tyndale.com, or call 1-855-277-9400.

**Library of Congress Cataloging-in-Publication Data**
Names: Alpern, Dave, author. | Thomas, David, date- author.
Title: Taking the lead : winning business principles that fuel Joe Gibbs racing / Dave Alpern with David Thomas.
Description: Carol Stream, Illinois : Tyndale Momentum, [2021] | Includes bibliographical references.
Identifiers: LCCN 2021007226 (print) | LCCN 2021007227 (ebook) | ISBN 9781496444578 (trade paperback) | ISBN 9781496444585 (kindle edition) | ISBN 9781496444592 (epub) | ISBN 9781496444608 (epub)
Subjects: LCSH: Success in business. | Success—Psychological aspects. | Joe Gibbs Racing (Firm)
Classification: LCC HF5386 .A5438 2021 (print) | LCC HF5386 (ebook) | DDC 650.1—dc23
LC record available at https://lccn.loc.gov/2021007226
LC ebook record available at https://lccn.loc.gov/2021007227

Printed in the United States of America

| 27 | 26 | 25 | 24 | 23 | 22 | 21 |
|----|----|----|----|----|----|----|
| 7  | 6  | 5  | 4  | 3  | 2  | 1  |

# Contents

Foreword by Joe Gibbs      ix

Prologue      1

**PRINCIPLE 1   Deliver More Than You Cost**

CHAPTER 1   The Power of Influence      7

CHAPTER 2   Make Yourself Indispensable      19

CHAPTER 3   Be a Fountain, Not a Drain      29

CHAPTER 4   Be a Complement, Not a Clone      39

**PRINCIPLE 2   Create a Winning Culture**

CHAPTER 5   Honoring God First and Foremost      51

CHAPTER 6   From Family Business to Factory      65

CHAPTER 7   Fitting the Joe Mold      77

CHAPTER 8   Buying In to a Culture of Yes      93

**PRINCIPLE 3   Stay on Mission**

CHAPTER 9   The Most Important Question      113

CHAPTER 10   People Fulfill the Mission      127

CHAPTER 11   A Mission-Critical Partner      137

CHAPTER 12   The Last Plane Out of Vietnam      149

**PRINCIPLE 4   Treat People as Souls, Not Transactions**

CHAPTER 13   People before Profits      159

CHAPTER 14   Conflict, Hard Messages, and Crisis      169

CHAPTER 15   Business Is Relationships      185

CHAPTER 16   Traits of the Greats      197

**PRINCIPLE 5**  **Win at Life**

CHAPTER 17   Achieving That Elusive Work-Life Balance   209

CHAPTER 18   Investing Most in Who Matters Most   221

CHAPTER 19   Not the Same Ol' J.D.   231

CHAPTER 20   Carrying on J.D.'s Legacy   243


Afterword   251

Acknowledgments   255

Notes   257

About the Authors   258

# Foreword

ONE OF MY EARLIEST MEMORIES of Dave Alpern comes from a football game outside my house involving my son J.D. and a group of his friends. As head coach of the NFL's Washington Redskins at the time, I was accustomed to quickly evaluating players.

I surveyed the players in that friendly game, and Dave stood out. He was skinny and probably weighed thirty pounds less than anyone else on our snow-covered lawn, but he impressed me with how he wasn't backing down at all.

*This kid is really competitive*, I thought.

I've known Dave since he was a teenager in J.D.'s closest circle of friends. I've also known him as a young man, a developing leader, and now as president of our race team, Joe Gibbs Racing. At each step in that progression, Dave has impressed me.

Dave was among my first hires—as an unpaid intern—when we started our team in 1991. I hired him alongside J.D. and Todd Meredith, another member of that friend group. None of them had specific assignments, but over time they naturally developed into complementary roles for which they were individually gifted. Along with Don Meredith, my business partner, and Jimmy Makar, my first crew chief and NASCAR expert, they helped JGR grow from eighteen employees and one car to our current staff of more than five hundred employees and nine cars competing in three stock car series.

We started JGR with the hope that our one car would have a chance to win races. Thirty years later, we have far exceeded those initial hopes, winning seven series championships, including five in NASCAR's top series. The number one reason we developed into one of NASCAR's top teams is because of great people. Dave Alpern is one of those.

As you will read in this book, Dave started as a gofer. On his own initiative, he became an expert at licensed products and led our young company into opportunities we did not know existed. He later moved into other front-office positions. In February 2016, he became our president.

The circumstances were difficult. My son J.D. had held that position, but he was struck with a rare disease. I started JGR as a family business to share with my two sons. (My youngest, Coy, is JGR's vice chairman and chief operating officer.) Dave was the clear choice to step into the presidency. And he has led us well.

Four reasons come to mind for Dave's success as a leader.

First, Dave possesses unusual wisdom. More specifically, he possesses *godly* wisdom. That is why even when he was known around JGR as "the T-shirt guy" because of his licensing work, I didn't hesitate to bring him into important decisions for our growing company. Now, many of those types of decisions run across his desk as our president.

Second, Dave has a gift for developing relationships. That is an important gift because I believe business is about relationships. Racing wouldn't exist as we know it without sponsors. I brought Dave into our relationships with sponsors long before that was part of his official job description because I noticed how good he was with people. JGR typically has thirty major sponsors at any given time. That's thirty important relationships for our company, and Dave's gift shines in that area.

Third, Dave is loyal. He has been loyal to our company since his first day on the job. And he was especially loyal to J.D. during his illness.

Few people will ever know how much Dave helped my son behind the scenes as J.D.'s disease progressed. In fact, when it became apparent that someone needed to officially take over J.D.'s responsibilities and we chose Dave, he struggled with the idea of becoming our president, because it meant replacing J.D. Dave cares about JGR and our people, and he has devoted his entire career to us. He provides us with a great sense of comfort because we know that he comes to work every day desiring to do what is best for our team and our people.

Fourth, Dave represents the values of Joe Gibbs Racing. He describes those values in detail in this book, offering the unique perspective of a non-family member who worked his way from unpaid intern to president of a family business. As you learn what those values are and how we make them work in our professional environment, I would like to add that Dave exemplifies all that you will read.

I am glad Dave wrote this book. He is part of the group that helped build our team from start-up to the success we now enjoy. I am honored he decided to provide this insight to the team we started. But more than that, I am proud to call Dave a friend and a member of my family.

*Joe Gibbs*

# Prologue

*ALL RIGHT. I'M GOOD WITH THIS.*

I stacked the pages neatly on top of each other.

Ten minutes.

How to sum up my best friend's life in only ten minutes? To do his life justice in that amount of time. To articulate how I felt about the friend I admired more than any other.

I'd had two weeks since his death to write the eulogy even though we had known for months this day was nearing. I had tried several times to turn my thoughts into words, but not until a week before the memorial service could I actually put pen to paper.

"Everybody sounds better at their eulogy than they really were," I told a friend. "But not J.D."

J.D. Gibbs was everything good that I could think to say about him and more.

He had been my moral compass since seventh grade. The person who helped lead me to my faith through the way he lived out his. The leader who brought me into the family business when I was neither family nor qualified. The man who served as my picture of what it means to be a Christian father.

So much to say, but so unsure of how to say it.

My father had died nine years earlier. I eulogized him, too. Writing

J.D.'s eulogy was more difficult than writing my dad's—and that had been difficult enough. A son eulogizing his father seems natural. Our dads are supposed to die at some point, and we, their sons, are to honor them. That's how aging works. But J.D. was forty-nine. A best friend isn't supposed to die so young. Especially a best friend like J.D.

I had spent much of the past two weeks reflecting on how in 1992 J.D. and his father, Joe—then the head coach of the NFL's Washington Redskins—had hired me as an unpaid intern when they started Joe Gibbs Racing. And how, as I advanced from intern to president, I witnessed the way our company grew into one of the premier franchises in all of sports. From working alongside a two-sport Hall of Famer in Coach Gibbs to partnering with some of the most successful companies in North America through their sponsorships with JGR, I had learned and developed business principles for what it takes to be the best. Not just the best company or even the best employee, but the best husband, father, and friend I could be.

I had learned that business, no different than life, is built on relationships. And no one I have known—no one—was more intentional about relationships than J.D. He had given so much to so many people. And yet he had so much more to give.

That's why his death—and his cruel illness of more than five years—made no sense. Even with all the faith I could muster, I still thought, *I just don't get this one.*

Two days before the memorial service, I finished my eulogy. Then I crumpled the papers and started all over. I wouldn't typically write out a speech to read word for word, but this time was different. It had to be. I owed it to J.D. not to get too emotional as I spoke.

I could hear him laughing. Poking fun at me. Just like he would when he walked past my office door.

*Pern, don't you turn into a blubbering idiot when you're up there talking about me.*

But more than that, I recognized the opportunity awarded to me.

The opportunity to honor J.D. in front of his wife. The opportunity to make sure his four sons understood how great a man and a friend their father was. And the opportunity to share the importance of J.D.'s faith on his behalf, because J.D. was always sharing his faith. Eulogizing my best friend was one of the most important responsibilities I had ever been given.

The night before the memorial service, I timed myself as I read aloud through the final version.

Ten minutes.

Finally convinced that I had used those minutes wisely, I laid the stack of papers on the desk and released a deep sigh of relief.

The question that guided me through the process of writing the eulogy was the same one I had employed since taking over J.D.'s job as president of Joe Gibbs Racing. And it is the same question that guides me today as I try to lead our company based on the principles that allowed us to grow into the winningest team in NASCAR history.

*How would J.D. handle this?*

PRINCIPLE 1

# DELIVER MORE THAN YOU COST

## Chapter 1

# THE POWER
# OF INFLUENCE

KYLE BUSCH HAD JUST WON the 2019 NASCAR Cup Series championship to cap our greatest season ever. The title was Kyle's second and the fifth in the history of Joe Gibbs Racing. Kyle's championship-clinching victory at Homestead-Miami Speedway was the nineteenth race win of the season for Joe Gibbs Racing. Four cars, nineteen victories out of thirty-six races—the most for any team in NASCAR's modern era.

I could not imagine a more emotional ending to our first season since the death of J.D. Gibbs, the son of team owner Joe Gibbs, my best friend, and the man I had replaced as president almost four years before in the early stages of his illness. As Kyle crossed the finish line to complete our dream season, his pit erupted in celebration. But instead of running straight to Victory Lane, I hurried down pit lane to catch the guys on our team who *weren't* celebrating—Erik Jones, Martin Truex Jr., and Denny Hamlin.

A unique juxtaposition exists from leading multiple race car teams that contend against one another. On the night Kyle's team won the championship, our other three teams lost. Like a parent with kids competing against each other, I hurt for each one who lost—the drivers, their crew members, and their sponsors. They are family.

Martin had won more races (seven) than any other driver in NASCAR that season. He finished second to Kyle in the championship race. Denny had won six races, and he had entered the final race as a popular favorite to win his first title because of his late-season momentum. Erik, who finished third in the race (and who was the only one of our drivers not in contention for the championship), was a young, up-and-coming driver with a bright future and one victory in 2019 to his credit.

Then there was the handful of executives from FedEx, which had sponsored Denny's number 11 car and requested that "#DoItForJD" be painted in purple letters across the car's back. How could I not root for the car honoring my best friend? Denny had come close to winning the championship twice before with FedEx, only to fall short both times. Obviously, I want all our drivers to perform well. But a first championship for Denny and FedEx, with their desire to honor J.D., would have made for a memorable conclusion to a historic year. Then with only forty-five laps to go in the race for the title—less than seventy miles—Denny experienced car trouble and had to settle for a fourth-place finish in the season standings.

I told Erik, Martin, and Denny that I was proud of them and thanked them for their contributions to our team's nineteen victories. I thanked the FedEx executives for their fifteen years of support and friendship. Then I joined Kyle's team in Victory Lane. The Mars (chocolate) family was there, along with all their top executives as the primary sponsor of Kyle's number 18 car. They are wonderful people, a family to us at JGR.

But when the championship celebration started to shift toward scattered locations, I wondered whether I should even post about our victory on social media out of consideration for Denny's and Martin's heartbreak.

To be clear: I definitely enjoyed being in Victory Lane for Kyle's team's moment. Being part of the immediate aftermath of the clinching win was awesome. That's the moment every team pursues throughout the nine-month grind of the NASCAR season. My disappointment amid that celebration was the welcome result of leading one of NASCAR's top teams.

Three of our drivers had earned spots among the "Championship 4" that arrived in Miami with an opportunity to leave as Cup champion. The annual goal is to place as many of your drivers into the final four as possible, and we became the first team ever to qualify three. But because we are a company built on relationships, even the crowning achievement in our sport came with disappointment mixed in.

Which is a lot like life. Most of life is a mixture of victories and defeats, often competing simultaneously for our emotions. Even when life seems easy, it can be difficult. But on this night, we won a championship and my family was with me, and I couldn't help but reflect on how far our team had come.

Joe Gibbs Racing's journey to a four-car, record-setting team started in 1991 with one car and a ton more hope than experience. I have been at JGR since the start, when the Gibbs family allowed me—a clueless, unconfident college graduate who had moved back home to live with his parents—to join their new company as an unpaid intern, happy to work out of an emptied broom closet with no electrical outlet (but a long extension cord). I have witnessed how a family business with eighteen employees grew to a championship team of around five hundred, and how every step in the process has come from a steadfast commitment to a simple mission: go fast.

And now as president of JGR, I help Coach Gibbs run that business. These days my office is larger and, fortunately, they pay me to work here. But the company-wide commitment to go fast remains the same.

When I reflect on JGR's history, I see five overarching principles that have guided us from nothing to greatness:

1. Deliver more than you cost.
2. Create a winning culture.
3. Stay on mission.
4. Treat people as souls, not transactions.
5. Win at life.

In addition to exploring each of these overarching principles, this book shares lessons within these principles that I have learned along the way. These lessons are keys to succeeding in business and in life. The pursuit of both is what makes Joe Gibbs Racing unique in our sport.

## Accepted into the Family

Starting out as an unpaid intern established a pretty low bar for delivering more than I cost. Heck, I just tried to stay out of the way most days. But from the beginning, I tried to create value for myself and earn my keep. Ultimately, delivering more than I cost is how I became the president of a family business without being in the family and why, thirty years later, I am still here. (And still not named Gibbs.)

But the story of how I became an unpaid intern at all is about the power of influence.

I met J.D. Gibbs in 1981 in middle school in Fairfax, Virginia, when his father, Joe, became head coach of my beloved Washington Redskins. The week after the Redskins lost to the San Francisco 49ers for an 0–5 start to Coach's first season, I invited J.D. to spend the night at my house. We joked that, based on the team's record, that might be the last time J.D. came over.

I recall that even though J.D. was living in a new city and already hearing angry fans speculating that his dad could be fired, he did not seem to have a care in the world. From seventh grade until the day he died, I never witnessed anything that could unsteady J.D. Even from an early age, his excited and depressed moods were no more than an inch apart.

By high school, J.D. held larger-than-life status to me. He was that guy who always seemed to do the right thing.

J.D. could have been created in a lab rather than born. He was good looking, he played quarterback on the varsity football team, and he had status and material possessions because of his dad's career. Yet his greatest enjoyment seemed to come from sharing his popularity with others. J.D. recognized the power of his influence and often sat at a cafeteria table with kids who weren't among the most popular or who belonged to a different social circle than his. He understood that with just a few words—"Hi, I'm J.D. How are you doing?"—he could make a positive impact on those kids who needed attention from a respected student-athlete like himself. And not once did I see J.D. take a seat at one of those tables and look over his shoulder to see who was watching.

> Others-focused leaders are motivated
> by seeing others succeed.

J.D. was my moral compass. From observing how he conducted himself in high school, I started asking myself, *How would J.D. handle this?* when I found myself in a situation I felt unprepared for.

The Gibbs home served as a popular hangout for the friends of J.D. and his younger brother, Coy. Coach was not there much during football seasons. I remember late nights when Coach would walk in around eleven o'clock or midnight after a long day at the Redskins' office. He loved his sons having friends over, and he would sit down and talk with us for a little bit before excusing himself to grab a few hours of sleep.

The Gibbs family also hosted weekly, biblically based meetings for a high school Young Life group. I accepted an invitation to one such meeting only because the offer came from a pretty girl. Plus, who wouldn't want to attend a party at the Redskins coach's house?

I did not grow up in church, and before I became a Christian, I wrongly considered Christianity a crock and Christians mentally weak people who had been brainwashed. But the pretty girl kept asking me to go, and I kept going.

J.D.'s home felt different from mine. By the time I entered high school, my dad had married his third wife. Dad was a former CIA agent who spoke multiple languages and had briefed presidents of the United States. The engineering firm he cofounded following his departure from the government almost instantly became successful with hundreds of employees. He was a gourmet chef, a brilliant pianist, and a big personality. Achievement was the chief pursuit in our family, and as the only son, I had a tough act to follow in my dad. He often told me, "You're going to do great things. You need to get great grades so you'll get into a great college." I wanted to make my dad proud, so accomplishments became my god. Except the accomplishments weren't coming.

In a high school of over three thousand students, I was by far the smallest boy in my freshman class at five feet tall and eighty-five pounds. I hadn't reached puberty yet. I had also been diagnosed with Tourette's syndrome in sixth grade. My symptoms got worse—of course—in high school. What a great one-two punch for making friends! As a teenage boy trying to fit in, battling those conditions and also chasing the god of great accomplishments to please my dad, I did not see much of a path to glory ahead for me.

Yet all throughout high school, J.D. treated me like I was the coolest guy in the world.

After graduation, J.D. and I attended different colleges but remained close friends. He moved on to the College of William & Mary in southeastern Virginia to play football. I stayed in Fairfax to attend George Mason University. Not that I preferred to stay close to home.

I planned to study electrical engineering to follow in my dad's footsteps, and my top three choices were Virginia, Virginia Tech, and Georgia Tech. None of those schools accepted me. Two of the rejection letters came on the same day. The dreaded thin envelope from a college admissions office was the telltale sign that you had received the one-page "Sorry to inform you" letter. I opened the two letters in the driveway and, before entering our house, detoured into the garage so I could fall to my knees and weep. I had no clue how I was going to tell my dad about the rejections, but I could hear those words he had said to me so many times.

*You need to get into a great college.*

I loved and respected my dad, and I didn't want to disappoint him. But I couldn't have felt like more of a failure. I wound up attending my fourth-choice school.

I can look back now and call my freshman year at George Mason the worst year of my life. Had I taken a ten-minute personality profile before college, I could have spared myself a miserable year in engineering. Before my sophomore year, I changed my major from engineering to mass communication and media studies. After finding a good academic fit, I helped found a fraternity. By staying home for college, I was able to be mentored by my Young Life leader, Rick Beckwith, and to grow in the faith I had come to call my own. I even became a volunteer Young Life leader at my old high school. Both helped me discover the untapped leadership potential I possessed. But most important, I met my wife, Stacey, during my sophomore year. George Mason proved to be the right place for me.

Staying in Fairfax also kept me in close contact with the Gibbs family.

Mrs. Gibbs would invite me and Moose Valliere, a close friend of mine and J.D.'s (and the future best man in my wedding), to sit in a luxury box with the family during Redskins games. Because J.D. was playing college football more than a two-hour drive away, I made it to more games than he did.

Coach had a ritual of hosting dinner at a local restaurant after his team's home victories. In that era of Redskins history, that meant after almost every home game. Coach invited his assistant coaches and family friends to the dinners. I felt both honored and unworthy to be among the invited.

I still remember the first time I attended one of those victory celebrations. I walked through the doors into a room filled with dozens of people. Before I had a chance to survey the crowd for anyone I recognized, Coach shouted, "Pern's here!" Then he walked directly to me, gave me a high five, and asked, "How about that game?"

Coach always made me feel special and like I was part of his family.

### Turning a Dream into Reality

The start of Joe Gibbs Racing is a right-time, right-place story. Coach had long held a dream of undertaking a business venture with J.D. and

Coy (younger by four years). Football seemed a natural fit, with Coy also playing in college at Stanford University. But J.D. had stated numerous times he would not get into coaching football professionally. Coach was well known for putting in long hours, typically sleeping in his office three nights a week during football season. J.D. had no desire to choose that lifestyle for his family, and Coach recognized that making his dream come true would require a shift on his part.

Coach grew up around auto racing in Southern California, and he owned a hot rod he raced on weekends in his younger days. In 1991, he and his boys decided to get into the racing business. Coach got into NASCAR, as they like to say in the South, while the getting was good. He entered on an uptick in NASCAR that led to *Sports Illustrated* declaring on one of its covers in 1995 that NASCAR was "America's hottest sport." If Coach had waited three or four years to start his team, the barrier to entry might have been too great.

When Coach joined NASCAR, he stepped into competing with car guys who had been in racing most or all of their lives—team owners like Roger Penske, Robert Yates, Jack Roush, and Rick Hendrick. Some were billionaires. Penske had bought, refurbished, and sold race cars as a teenager and then became a championship racer before achieving business icon status. Yates had built engines for cars that won seventy-seven races at NASCAR's top level before he formed his own team. Roush was a former drag and road racer who had worked as an engineer at Ford before creating a business that built engines for race teams. Hendrick became the youngest Chevrolet dealer in the country at age twenty-six, and his success led to the creation of a large network of auto dealerships. His Hendrick Motorsports team, established in 1984, became one of NASCAR's innovative leaders.

Although Coach had drag raced and loved cars, he would be the first to say he was not a car guy on a par with those he would compete against. Coach was a football guy—one of the best coaches ever, at any level—and he was about to take a full dive into discovering the differences between NASCAR and football.

Perhaps the biggest contrast between NASCAR and football is that the franchise model of football (and other team sports, for that matter) allows an owner to stay in business even if the team stinks. An NFL team can finish with a losing record season after season and its owner still turn a profit. I've heard Coach tell stories about going to NFL owners meetings, looking at the teams represented around the room, and crossing off about a third of the teams from having a legitimate chance to win based on the questions the teams' representatives asked and how they ran their businesses. They didn't seem to understand what was required to win in the NFL. But the teams in that room were making money because of the league's franchise model.

Coach quickly observed that wouldn't be the case with NASCAR. Race teams were not franchises, and those that did not win couldn't raise the money necessary to stay in business. There would be no handouts, no guarantees from the league. Owners like Penske, Hendrick, and Roush owned mega-successful businesses. I don't know if they ever covered for their race teams' down periods with income from their other businesses, but we assumed they could if needed. Coach's team could not. He made good money for an NFL coach, but he didn't make enough to float an underfunded NASCAR team. From the first day, Joe Gibbs Racing would have to hunt for everything it ate.

NASCAR teams stay in business by obtaining and retaining sponsorships. Sponsors are the lifeblood of NASCAR. Currently, 80 percent of our income is from sponsorships. If Joe Gibbs Racing could not secure a sponsor in its early days, Coach's dream for him and his sons would never make it to a track.

Coach had to sell the belief that because he had won in football, he could and would win in NASCAR.

To start his team, he paired with a trusted friend, Don Meredith (not the quarterback), who had partnered with Coach on ministry ventures. They targeted five companies to which they wanted to pitch the idea of sponsoring the team.

Coach's second pitch was to Interstate Batteries. Norm Miller was—

and still is—Interstate's chairman. Coach met with Norm in Dallas, Texas, at the site of Interstate's headquarters.

"Who's your driver?" Norm asked Coach.

"We don't have one," Coach replied.

"Where's your building?" Norm asked.

"We don't have one."

"What manufacturer are you using? Are you using Chevy? Ford?"

"You don't understand," Coach said. "This is literally a dream on a sheet of paper."

Coach returned home realizing how ridiculous the venture he was attempting to undertake was. As he reviewed his meeting with Norm, Coach concluded, *He must think I'm nuts*. The next day, Coach called Norm to apologize for wasting his time.

Norm interrupted Coach before he could issue the apology. "You know, it's funny," Norm said. "We were going to call you today. I think we're going to do this."

With a sponsor secured to provide funding, Coach spent his short NFL off-season making trips to Charlotte, North Carolina, where the majority of NASCAR teams made their homes. Coach met with representatives from various teams to ask, "Who would you like to have on your team?" Coach compiled a list of names and started researching. And then he did what Coach does as well as anyone: recruit. Coach is the quintessential recruiter, because he can sell people on an idea and the opportunity to be part of a winning culture.

His first target was a driver: Dale Jarrett. Dale possessed NASCAR pedigree and an enviable future. At thirty-five, he had raced five full seasons in the Cup Series. His dad, Ned Jarrett, had won two championships at NASCAR's highest level and, at the time, was a color analyst of NASCAR races for CBS and ESPN. Ned has since been inducted into the NASCAR Hall of Fame. Dale had grown up in racing.

When Coach contacted him, Dale was in the last year of a contract with Wood Brothers Racing, which had fielded a NASCAR team since

1950. Ned held a long friendship with Eddie and Len Wood, second-generation owners of the team. On top of that, Jarrett was driving the number 21 car long associated with the likes of David Pearson, Neil Bonnett, Buddy Baker, and Kyle Petty. Dale had not won a race yet—he would later that season—but the combination of Jarrett and the Wood Brothers seemed to be a team bursting with promise.

Coach could have pursued more prominent drivers, but Dale was relatively young and a high-character guy who would represent a company well. Not being under contract for 1992 also made Dale a candidate to drive for Coach in his team's first season.

Coach made his pitch to Dale, who asked his brother-in-law, Jimmy Makar, his opinion of joining the upstart team. Makar, who had worked in NASCAR about fifteen years and had recently become a crew chief, advised Dale, "It wouldn't hurt you to go there. But I'm not leaving for there."

Dale decided to leave a team with a rich history in NASCAR to drive with a team that barely existed.

Naturally, Coach's second hire was Makar, who left Penske Racing South midseason to accept Coach's offer to become his crew chief—his car guy—and to take on the task of filling out the remainder of his fifteen-person team.

Makar hired all but three of those fifteen: J.D.; Todd Meredith, Don's son; and me. Todd was a friend of mine and J.D.'s who had recently completed his accounting degree. Todd, J.D., and I were unique and complementary to each other in our giftings. We must have been created to be a team of three.

I had wound up on the four-and-a-half-year college plan and graduated the previous December. I had great friends and an amazing girlfriend in Stacey, whom I wanted to marry. But I was also living with my parents and working at a Nordstrom store in the mall with no real career plans other than an interest in broadcast journalism. I still felt like a failure who was letting my dad down.

With Coach leading the Redskins, J.D. said JGR needed someone who could drive memorabilia signed by Coach back and forth between Northern Virginia, where I lived, and the race team's new office in Charlotte. He offered me the job with a $500 stipend to cover expenses. Any pay would still have to come from my part-time job at the mall. I was hoping to find a full-time job somewhere, but J.D.'s offer seemed like it might later provide a chance.

J.D. could have made the offer to many of his friends, but he picked me, he said, because I was reliable and because he and Coach could count on me. Their hiring me—even though I was basically a gofer making eight-hundred-mile round trips—felt like a bright red stamp on me reading "APPROVED." I realized that in many ways, the manner in which I had handled myself as friends with J.D. had unknowingly served as my audition for this job, and the influence he had—as my friend and as someone I looked up to—served to change the course of my life.

## TOPICS FOR REFLECTION

1. J.D.'s influence in my life helped me to gain confidence and eventually led to my being invited to join Joe Gibbs Racing at the ground floor. Who has been influential in your life? How did they gain that influence? In what ways has their influence made you a better you?

2. J.D.'s influence was often as simple as sitting with people who were lonely or making others feel wanted or approved. Consider your sphere of influence—home, work, school, church, your neighborhood. Can you think specifically of someone in each circle who might need encouragement or who could benefit from your influence? What steps could you take today or in the coming week to use your influence to benefit others?

## Chapter 2

# MAKE YOURSELF INDISPENSABLE

J.D., Todd, and I liked to think of ourselves as a modern-day three musketeers who were beckoned to save the day for JGR. Jimmy Makar had his own name for us: "the three college pukes."

I said that Jimmy Makar was Coach's second hire. Actually, he was the second hire who *stayed*. Coach had hired a general manager before Jimmy, but he didn't last long. Coach brought in J.D., Todd, and me to replace the general manager, pretty much telling Jimmy, "Here are your guys. Figure out what to do with them."

There are two Jimmy Makars. Today, Jimmy is one of the kindest, most laid-back guys anyone could meet. But in those early days, Jimmy was known as "Mad Dog." Trust me, Jimmy earned that nickname. Mad Dog had a short fuse to a hot temper. No one outworked Jimmy, and he held high expectations for everyone around him. If you landed on Jimmy's bad side, he would let you know in the most direct manner possible, except for a few detours to mix in some choice profanities.

Jimmy terrified me. I didn't know if Jimmy could fire us, because

19

Coach had hired us, but I didn't want to find out. I also knew that Jimmy was only tolerating us "pukes." I probably would rather have been fired than cussed out by Jimmy. Wanting to stay on Jimmy's good side as much as possible—plus stay the heck out of his way—I determined to create a need for me at JGR.

Coach was revered around Washington, DC (and still is). The nation's capital is a city sharply divided by politics, but the Washington Football Team possesses the power to unite the city during football season. That's a common dynamic between many sports cities and their teams, but because of what Washington, DC, represents on the world's political stage, I cannot imagine a more significant team-to-city relationship. When the team is good, life is grand in DC. When the Redskins were among the NFL's elite teams under Coach—he had led them to four Super Bowls at that point—there was no better place to be on a Sunday afternoon than RFK Stadium, then home of the Redskins. Beyond game days, the atmosphere around the city was electric throughout the entire football season. Coach was so popular that he would walk into a restaurant and diners would start clapping and sometimes give him a standing ovation.

I noted how much signed Coach Gibbs memorabilia I was driving back and forth to Charlotte and how anything with "Joe Gibbs" on it seemed in high demand. An idea struck me that I presented to J.D.: print Joe Gibbs Racing shirts and sell them at RFK Stadium. Forget that I had no idea how or where to print T-shirts and that this was pre-internet days, when *Google* wasn't a synonym for *research*.

I researched the name of the Redskins' head buyer, a man named Jim, and tracked down his number. Amazingly, I reached him on the phone and he accepted a meeting with me. Off I went, making my first sales call with a sample T-shirt in hand.

"I'm here on behalf of Coach Gibbs," I said. (I'm no dummy— I understood the only reason he agreed to meet.) "Would you be interested in setting up a kiosk at the stadium that sells these T-shirts?"

I explained how I would bring one case of seventy-two shirts in various sizes and sell the shirts on consignment. Jim would assume no risk. He would make money on the T-shirts that sold and give back the remainders.

"Coach wants to personally thank you for considering this," I added.

I left Jim's office with the deal finalized. My first business deal! Jim asked for "a PO," and with no clue what one of those was, I assured him, "I'll get it to you when I get back to the office." Then I returned to my office, which was my dad's house, where I had no computer and no printer, and I still did not know that a "PO" was a purchase order.

When I updated J.D. and Don on my meeting, I omitted the part about selling the shirts on consignment. I was convinced the shirts would sell. If not, I would pay for the shirts out of my own pocket, even though there was little in that pocket.

All seventy-two T-shirts sold at the first game of the season. Jim ordered more, and that one day propelled JGR—and me!—into the T-shirt business. I had created a need for myself in the company, and just like that, I became known around Joe Gibbs Racing as "the T-shirt guy." The simple T-shirt idea, it turned out, launched my career and taught me the importance of making myself indispensable.

> Create value for yourself in your company
> by making yourself indispensable.

After the shirts' success, I wanted to create more opportunities. We developed a plan to go to the NFL to obtain the rights to sell denim NFL jackets that were not NASCAR-related. I started making phone calls concerning other potential revenue ideas, particularly in licensing. The funny thing was that I didn't know how licensing worked. I had to figure it all out.

After six months of running a part-time licensing business from my parents' house while still working at the mall and thinking of a future with Stacey, the conditions seemed right for serious soul-searching. I needed something full-time, and my JGR job wasn't quite there yet.

I had remained an active part of Young Life, taking on increasing leadership roles as I grew in my own faith. Rick Beckwith, our Young Life leader, had become a much-needed mentor, and he and I talked numerous times about my going on staff at Young Life. Leading in Young Life brought me a sense of fulfillment, but my dad was more skeptical of Christianity than I had been, and I feared what he would think if I went to work full-time for a ministry.

I had reached a critical crossroads in my life, and I was not sensing what direction I should head. So I set a date of March 1, 1992, and consistently prayed that the route I should go would become clear by that date.

On March 2, a Monday, with my self-imposed deadline come and gone and still lacking direction, I was sitting in my house dejected. I called Stacey to vent.

"I don't understand," I told her in tears. "I've been faithful, and God went silent on me. Why won't he just show me what I'm supposed to do?"

Stacey tried to lift my spirits and encouraged me to remain faithful. Those were the days of landlines and call-waiting, and the phone clicked with an incoming call.

"This might be my answer," I told Stacey.

I clicked over to the other call. Don Meredith was calling from JGR headquarters.

"We just signed a new sponsor that will require us to have someone at Joe Gibbs Racing to handle the account and do the day-to-day servicing for them. We talked about it, and we all think you would be perfect. Can you be in Charlotte on Monday to start?"

"Yes, sir," I replied. "I'll be there on Monday."

I immediately called Stacey back.

"I got my answer," I informed her. "I'm moving to Charlotte, hon! This is my chance!"

## Humble Beginnings

To call my first office a broom closet is no exaggeration.

Todd dressed up the closet for me before my arrival, removing all the cleaning supplies and adding black trim along the bottoms of the walls. My desk was an elementary school desk with an attached plastic chair. Since there were no electrical outlets, my small lamp was plugged into an extension cord. I had a phone with a long cord, but who in the world would I call? The only other item on my desk was a spiral notebook. My office had no chair for a guest, because there was no room for a guest; I had to walk into the hallway to hold a meeting. But I was in business. I was now a full-time employee for Joe Gibbs.

The new job did not come with a salary, at least for the few first months. J.D. and Todd shared an apartment, and they let me live with them and sleep on the floor. I rotated from one bedroom floor to the other a week at a time. Considering I had no bedroom to call my own, having a broom closet for an office wasn't the worst thing in the world.

I traveled to races every other weekend. The other weekends, I drove the six hours to Virginia on Friday night to see Stacey and was back in Charlotte for work by Monday morning.

Two companies helped me land the job in Charlotte. The first was Mark III Vans, the sponsor Don had called about that needed an account rep. They were a van conversion company that took stock vans, placed televisions and wood paneling inside, and sold them. The company was expanding into sports with plans to sell vans with imaging of fans' favorite NASCAR drivers and NFL teams. I would go to half of the races on the NASCAR schedule and serve as the boots-on-the-ground rep to roll out the business. Coach Gibbs was serving as a spokesman for the company, and he had agreed to help sign up all the other drivers. With that came my services: to basically be a gofer for them at the track to help with whatever was needed to get the deal off the ground.

The second company was, fittingly, a T-shirt company—a national licensed-apparel company named Nutmeg Mills.

Brothers Marty and Dick Jacobson ran Nutmeg Mills. Both are great guys, and Marty to this day serves on our advisory board and is a dear friend of Joe's. Nutmeg, which made apparel for pro sports leagues, reached out to Coach about getting involved with NASCAR. To that point, NASCAR merchandise was sold only at tracks or in small specialty stores. Unlike other sports, NASCAR did not (and still does not) have centralized licensing. A company wanting to make NFL T-shirts, for example, could make a deal with the league office for all NFL teams. In NASCAR, a deal would need to be made with each driver separately. That process could be cumbersome.

Coach recognized the huge opportunity Nutmeg presented and worked out a deal that made Nutmeg the first apparel company to take NASCAR to national retail. Coach agreed to help Nutmeg secure contracts with our sport's top drivers. Coach was so sure the deal would work that in lieu of an endorsement fee, he asked for a small percentage of total sales. Coach hit a home run on that deal, because he signed up the big-name drivers for Nutmeg, including Dale Earnhardt Sr., Jeff Gordon, Rusty Wallace, and Bill Elliott. And guess who became the gofer?

One of my first assignments with Nutmeg involved going to Atlanta Motor Speedway on a Friday, which was arrival day for the Cup drivers, and coordinating a photo shoot of each driver wearing his T-shirt and hat for a catalog. I had to iron the shirts, carry them on hangers through the garage, find each driver's PR guy, and then get the driver to slip on the shirt and hat and pose with his hauler as the backdrop. Nobody had any idea who I was, and I looked about sixteen years old, so you can imagine how impressed the drivers were with me. I managed to get photos for every driver that first day but one, Earnhardt. I already was terrified of meeting "The Intimidator," as he was known because of his aggressive driving style. Then he crashed his car in practice. Let's just say he was in no mood for T-shirt photos. Much to my relief, we ended up making a computer-generated shot of Earnhardt wearing his hat.

I am grateful to both of those companies, because their partnerships with Joe Gibbs Racing provided my ticket in. Nutmeg wound up partnering with us for over a decade until being sold to a larger clothing conglomerate. I still consider Marty—and his son, Matt—a great friend and brilliant marketing mind.

Even with two "official" clients within the company, I was still looking for ways to increase my value for JGR. I booked hotel rooms. I helped with show cars we displayed at publicity events. And, yes, I spent a lot of time on T-shirts.

The paychecks started within a few months of my move to Charlotte, but I wasn't making much. I traveled extensively, alternating between races and going home to see Stacey. I didn't know how long my gig would last, but I liked my job. I was working and living with two of my best friends, and the owner of the company happened to be my idol. We could have been selling coat hangers, and it wouldn't have mattered. The *who* has always been more important than the *what* to me.

Little did I know what was in store for me over the next three decades. I can appreciate even more where JGR is today because I was around for the humble beginnings. And believe me, they were humble.

## Finally, a Checkered Flag

We didn't win a single race our first season, 1992. Oh-for-twenty-nine. We finished second at Bristol Motor Speedway early in the season and came in third in the Pepsi 400, the midseason race at Daytona International Speedway. Interstate Batteries was patient with us; they held realistic expectations for a first-year team. But still, we wanted to make our sponsor happy. In NASCAR, that means earning as much TV airtime as possible by winning races and leading laps. We finished that initial season with zero wins and barely more than a hundred laps led.

When we did win for the first time, we made it a big one. One of NASCAR's unique aspects among professional sports is that it opens the season with its showcase event, the Daytona 500. That would be like the NFL airing the Super Bowl in its first week.

In the 1992 Daytona 500, our first race, Dale Jarrett had placed thirty-sixth out of forty-two cars, crashing out less than halfway into the race. At Daytona in 1993, Dale was running the number 18 Interstate Batteries car solidly in third place late in the race. He passed twenty-one-year-old rookie Jeff Gordon with two laps to go to move into second. Then on the last lap, he slipped past leader Dale Earnhardt Sr. and held off the then-five-time champion all the way to the finish line.

As part of our licensing agreement with the NFL then, we had decided that for each race, Dale Jarrett would wear a helmet painted to look like an NFL team's helmet. Most races, we picked the NFL team geographically closest to that race. For Daytona, we selected a Dallas Cowboys helmet for Dale, because the Cowboys had won the Super Bowl the previous week. Plus, with Interstate's headquarters in Dallas, the Cowboys helmet added a nice touch for our sponsor for our biggest race.

Coach was still head coach of the Redskins and about a month short of announcing his retirement from coaching football. The Cowboys are the Redskins' archnemesis, and when Dale crossed the finish line, Coach sent an urgent message that Dale needed to remove that Cowboys helmet before he climbed out of his car in Victory Lane. There was no way Coach was going to allow the lasting photo of his team's first win to be his driver with the Cowboys star on the sides of his helmet.

Unseen by the TV cameras was the relief on J.D.'s face when Dale won. J.D. and Todd were members of the pit crew, and J.D.'s first race as a tire changer was that Daytona 500. After Dale's final pit stop, J.D. told Todd and me that on one of his tires, he had fully tightened only three of the five lug nuts. Based on experience, my immediate thought was to fear how Mad Dog would react.

"Are you going to tell Jimmy?" I asked.

"Heck, no," J.D. said.

"Do you think Dale can make it to the end?" Todd asked.

"We're about to find out," J.D. answered.

Fortunately, the lug nuts held.

## TOPICS FOR REFLECTION

1. It was clear to me early in my time at Joe Gibbs Racing that the best way to prove my value was to make myself indispensable by creating my own niche within the company. Think about your own job. What part of your job would your organization have a difficult time hiring someone else to do?

2. I was the T-shirt guy, the gofer, the "whatever needed to be done" guy for many years. What are some specific ways you might be able to make yourself indispensable in your organization?

## Chapter 3

# BE A FOUNTAIN, NOT A DRAIN

THE MEMORIES OF EARNING THAT first victory in the biggest race of them all remain so fresh that sometimes it's difficult to realize that moment was more than twenty-five years ago. Now, Joe Gibbs Racing owns four Cup teams, employs more than five hundred people, and is the winningest team in NASCAR history in the top two series, with over three hundred fifty wins. Add to that, while I still often think of myself as that unpaid intern, my business card actually reads "President."

I certainly did not see that coming as "the T-shirt guy" in 1993. I wasn't sure what kind of future I would have at JGR working in a family business and not being part of the family. I wanted to climb higher, but I couldn't envision that my ceiling in our small company was much higher than my position at the time.

I figured I had two choices: leave and find a job somewhere else with higher growth opportunities, or stay and find purpose in the menial tasks I was expected to perform.

Everyone has specific gifts and personal strengths. I believe there are few jobs that perfectly align with our gifts and strengths, where we are in our "sweet spot," where our passion and our skill set intersect 100 percent of the time. For most of us, a career is a balance of performing tasks we are good at and love and also of doing stuff we aren't that good at and don't like. That is especially true early in a career, as I experienced at JGR. The temptation in those situations is to think, *I'm above this task. This isn't using my gifts.* That is a temptation best rejected. Included in the principle of delivering more than you cost is *never* saying, "That's not my job."

I chose to find purpose in being the T-shirt guy. If that was my job, then I would become the best T-shirt guy in NASCAR history. I attended trade shows to learn more about marketing and licensing. I met other T-shirt folks in NASCAR and set up lunches with them and grilled them about their experiences. I made contact with the T-shirt guys for the NFL and Major League Baseball and learned from them.

The expectation for me within JGR was that I would print T-shirts featuring our driver. I could have done that well and stayed in good graces. Instead, I chose to discover the ins and outs of trademark licensing and the entire licensing industry.

My big-picture goal was that if Coach and J.D. met to evaluate the staff against a tight budget, they would both say, "If we have to get rid of someone, we can't get rid of Dave—he does way too much to have to replace him. He's indispensable."

To accomplish that goal, no one was going to hear me say, "That's not my job."

> The path to creating more value than you cost never includes saying, "That's not my job."

One day the team was behind schedule in their preparations for the next race, and as I was walking through the garage, I asked if anyone needed help. The next thing I knew, I was holding a razor blade, a squee-gee, and a hair dryer to place a decal on a car.

I'm almost helpless mechanically to begin with. I can assemble a piece of furniture if the instructions are clear, I can hang a picture in our home, and I can change a flat tire slowly. But that's about it. My brain does not function like a mechanic's, and I don't enjoy fixing the few things I am capable of fixing. Feeling out of place as a front office guy work-ing among the mechanics and self-conscious of how long I had been in the car guys' way, I was sweating from the stress over the air bubbles. Mercifully, I received a quick decal application tutorial: a tiny razor cut on a bubble followed by the application of heat from the hair dryer and a smooth wipe with the squeegee pushed the air right out. Who knew?

How much I actually helped in that instance was debatable. Guys were practically tripping over me trying to work on the car as I waged war against air bubbles trapped behind the decal. But even my strug-gling to stick a decal on a car brought value, because with a race coming up and the whole team in catch-up mode, my taking on the decal work allowed the car guys to do the jobs that only car guys could do. I could have walked through the garage, noted the pace of my coworkers as they tried to catch up, and said, "Hey, I went to college. I'm a marketing guy; I ain't doing that. I'll go back to my office." Or when given my task, I could have replied, "I don't do decals." Those types of thoughts went through my mind on many occasions, but I didn't indulge them.

Refusing to submit to the "That's not my job" temptations did not apply only to the garage, where my skills were clearly limited. I chose to also take that approach in the front office.

Sponsorships were not part of my job description, but I was an extrovert and good at building relationships. Even as the T-shirt guy at races, I made a point of initiating relationships with our sponsors. As those relationships grew, sponsors started confiding in me ways that JGR could be better. I passed that feedback along to Coach, and he made changes to bring more benefit to our sponsors.

After a few of those conversations, Coach started pointing out people within our sponsoring companies that I needed to develop relationships with. As those relationships grew, some of my sponsor contacts began treating me as their primary point of contact. That led to me doing more work for which I wasn't being paid!

I knew of meetings with potential sponsors, and I would be in a back room working on a T-shirt, stewing that I wasn't in the front room with Coach, J.D., and the potential partner. Sometimes I paced the hallway outside the conference room, telling myself, *I should be in there! I want to be a part of selling these big companies on the vision of JGR!* Right or wrong, that's how I felt. I wanted to make my area of the company so important, to make myself so indispensable, that Coach would have to invite me into the next meeting.

During one such meeting, Coach's assistant, Cindy Mangum, watched me pacing and asked, "What in the world are you doing, Pern?" I vented, "Next time Coach has a sponsor meeting, I'd love to be invited. I can talk about my area. I mean, licensed products are a big deal." I had also learned early who held influence in the office, and nobody had more than Coach's assistant, Cindy! (And that's still true to this day.)

After the meeting, Coach came looking for me and said, "Yeah, your area is a big deal. Why don't you join the next sponsor meeting we have?" Boom! (And thank you, Cindy!)

In internal meetings to talk about licensed products, I took the opportunity to interject how the company could get more value out of the sponsorship. For the next meeting with a potential sponsor, Coach made sure I was there. By excelling in smaller things, I had earned the right to be in those meetings where Coach was asking another company for millions of dollars. What wasn't my job eventually became part of my responsibilities because over time I built up trust and proved competence by not saying "That's not my job" to tasks I didn't want to do.

## Lost Presentation, Lost Job?

JGR was involved with the National Hot Rod Association for a few years, and my first presentation for the company came in 1994 as we started our drag racing team.

A small group of us flew to California to pitch a significant sponsorship to a company that made computer chips. In the pre-PowerPoint, old-school days of presentations, we paid a small fortune to a graphics specialist who created a visual for our pitch. We painted an actual drag race car with potential graphics and shipped the car ahead of us to be on display at the meeting site. Paper graphics of all our car designs and driver uniforms made up a critical visual element of my speech. I took the copies of the presentation with me in a cardboard box.

After we arrived at the hotel, a bellhop loaded my bags onto a cart and took them to my room. When I unpacked my luggage, I did not have the cardboard box of presentation materials. That realization occurred at the exact moment Coach called my room and said, "Let's get together and review the presentation."

"Uhhhhh," I said, scanning the room, "okay."

I tore up my room looking for the box. Not there. I ran down to the front desk. No one there remembered seeing the box or knew where it could be.

*What in the world am I going to tell Coach?*

I heard his response in my thoughts: "What have I done? I've put a twenty-five-year-old kid in charge of the biggest and most expensive presentation we've ever made, and he lost the entire thing!"

Coach came to my room, and I confessed to losing the presentation. He didn't say what I anticipated. But to this day, I still believe there was a good chance he thought it.

I went to bed that night trying to figure out what we would do for our presentation. I simultaneously wondered if Coach would fire me. My mind raced with emergency ideas including hand gestures and puppets to communicate our plan.

When I woke up the next morning, I spotted the flashing red light on the phone beside my bed. I dialed in for the message.

"Mr. Alpern, we have your missing box down at the front desk."

The box had fallen off the bellhop's cart in the elevator, and a hotel guest took it to the front desk. My first business trip to give a presentation sparked a new policy at JGR: a presentation never leaves our hands.

We ended up securing a small deal with the company—not the one we wanted, but a deal nonetheless. My building up trust of ownership and value happened by making lots of deposits over a period of time, with a few withdrawals too. Like almost losing a big presentation.

**Fountains and Drains**

When I speak in college business classes, I advise students, "Be a fountain, not a drain." Are you breathing life into every transaction, or sucking the life out of it?

We hold 100-percent control over whether we will be a fountain or a drain. It's our choice, not a result of our circumstances.

My office has a large glass window, and I can see someone a second before they arrive at my door. A drain is the person who, when I see them cross in front of my window, causes me to brace myself, roll my eyes, and mutter, "This is going to hurt." They are likely to walk into my office with complaints about how a problem is not their fault while having no interest in providing a solution. Whether it's a two- or fifteen-minute conversation, that person is going to drain energy from me.

Then there are the fountains. When I see them cross in front of my window, I leap up from my chair to meet them at the door because I know they are about to breathe life into me.

Fountains are encouragers. They usually are people with a high emotional IQ. They understand how to empathize and how to communicate well, and they know when to motivate and when to listen. Fountains are the employees who ask their coworkers, "How can I help you?" Fountains, ultimately, are the most valuable people in an organization because they make everyone around them better.

> Fountains bring value to a company by making everyone around them better.

Let me be clear that you can have a stressful job or even deliver bad news and still be a fountain. An ER doctor, a firefighter, and an entry-level administrator can be fountains. It's about going into every interaction with a posture of optimism and encouragement and a mindset asking, "How can I add value to this conversation and leave the people I'm interacting with better off than they were before?"

Anyone who has worked at Joe Gibbs Racing has heard Coach talk about Bucky. Bucky has been with us since day one with his signature paint sprayer in one hand and a cigarette in the other. (Dangerous combination, we know.)

Bucky's lungs might be Interstate Batteries bright green from all the years he painted that car before technology allowed us to go all decal. Coach talks frequently about Bucky not just because he is good at his job but because every interaction with Bucky fills people's tanks. He is encouraging and optimistic. He *never* complains, because he is content.

Although Bucky rarely enters the land of the front office, when I see him pass my window, I'm getting out of my chair to meet him. I know Bucky genuinely wants to know how I'm doing, how my family is doing, and how he can encourage us in the front office. Every Bucky interaction is too short, as though he values your time more than his own.

On the other hand, drains enter every interaction with a posture of defensiveness, finger-pointing, and gossiping. Few things suck the life out of me more than someone eager to share a big problem, toss in some gossip about whose fault it is, and leave without taking any responsibility or offering any solutions. Drains also can express themselves in smaller ways, such as

» shaking their head while someone is speaking, rather than nodding in affirmation;

» communicating with negative body language, such as slouching in a chair rather than sitting up and engaging in a conversation;

» displaying a lack of eye contact and a facial expression that screams, "I'd rather be anywhere but here"; and

» interrupting and raising their voice.

If someone is a drain, that usually spills over to their personal life and their social media. Every post is a complaint. "Traffic was so bad today." "Another delayed flight." "These people are morons."

A drain can sap the energy out of an entire company. So as we consider the principle of delivering more than you cost, remember that fountains add value to a company. Be a fountain, not a drain.

## Thinking, "You, You, You"

Interstate Batteries, the company responsible for us being in racing, exudes the trait of being a fountain. I can't think of a single person I know who works for Interstate Batteries who isn't a fountain. Being a fountain is woven into the fabric of their culture.

Every interaction with Interstate fills my tank, whether it is with Norm or Scott Miller, or with one of the racing guys who comes to the track. Their attitude is positive, even during difficult conversations. They always want to know how I'm doing and are quick to praise and compliment and slow to criticize.

In a world of "me, me, me" people, Interstate is loaded with "you, you, you" folks. I do not recall hearing anyone at Interstate take credit for something. They either want to make us look good or deflect praise to a coworker.

I save every handwritten note I receive, and I have a desk full of notes from Interstate Batteries. Many are from Charlie, their sponsorship guy, who to me has become much more than a sponsorship guy. Charlie is an encourager and uplifter, a fountain who is not interested in boosting himself; he would rather remind me of when I do something well. Charlie exemplifies the culture at Interstate and is proof of the impact being a fountain can have on those around you.

Observing Interstate Batteries for nearly thirty years has taught me so much about what it means to be a fountain—how setting up people around you to succeed and praising their success is not only admirable but also leads to a successful business. Interstate is not the number one aftermarket battery company in America by accident.

If I could write a playbook for students, I'd include what I learned from my friends at Interstate Batteries about becoming indispensable: shift your focus from "me, me, me" to "you, you, you."

Making others around you look good seems to have become increasingly difficult for young people. High school and college are one big competition. In academics and sports, and even socially, students have been taught to separate themselves, to stand out from the rest. Class rank determines what colleges they get into and what jobs they land. So why should a high school kid care about helping someone else rank higher than they do? If a scholarship is needed, why would an athlete help a teammate potentially outshine them? Elevate someone socially at their own expense? No way. When today's students enter the business world, it should come as no surprise that an others-first approach does not come naturally, and an employee tooting their own horn is counterproductive.

J.D. exemplified an others-focused mindset. Not once did he boast about one of his many achievements. Every encounter with J.D. started with a comment directed toward me like "What do you think about this, Pern?" or "That's a great idea."

In meetings, J.D. wasn't one of those people who loved to hear himself talk. He deflected to others. Knowing it would boost my confidence, he would say, "Dave, why don't you explain this?" He would respond to a compliment with "Actually, Dave put quite a bit of time on this too, and he deserves a lot of the credit." Those are small examples of a "you, you, you" posture in business, but I can say from my experience that they made a huge impact.

People who can make those around them better usually make the best employees and best leaders. And they exemplify the principle of delivering more than you cost.

## TOPICS FOR REFLECTION

1. Very few of us get to do what we're best at 100 percent of the time. Never saying "That's not my job" is a key way to deliver more than you cost. How do you feel when presented with a task that is outside your job or specialty? What steps can you take to develop a greater willingness to accept these tasks as they arrive?

2. There are some people who breathe energy into every interaction (fountains) and others who suck the energy out of interactions (drains). What are some characteristics of the fountains in your life? What makes being around fountains so energizing? How can you be more fountain-like in your interactions?

## Chapter 4

# BE A COMPLEMENT, NOT A CLONE

IN ORDER TO MAXIMIZE OUR VALUE to a company, it's easy to try to become what others want us to be. To impress the ones who assign us our value, including our bosses, we become who they think we should be. This idea makes sense, right?

It's a trap.

Trying to become who others want us to be ignores who we were *created* to be. Instead of reprogramming what we were wired to do, we need to be who we were created to be and do what we were created to do.

My dad was an engineer. I was pretty good at math, so I grew up thinking that becoming an electrical engineer was my lot in life. Yet two weeks into my freshman year as an electrical engineering major, I knew I had made a mistake. Engineering wasn't my thing.

My three sons are examples of how each person has different wiring, even within the same family. Our twins, Evan and Austin, are type A, off-the-chart extroverts, and high achievers who never want a quiet moment in their structured schedules. They recently started their careers in consulting post-graduation from the University of North Carolina at Chapel Hill's Kenan-Flagler Business School. They draw energy from people and from getting things done. They have a lot in common with their dad.

Collin, our youngest, is much more laid back. He is studying audio engineering at Belmont University in Nashville, Tennessee, with hopes of becoming a music producer. Collin has more of an artist's personality, preferring a loose schedule (like his mom). He enjoys margin in his life and would rather stay up late and wake up late. He's a peacemaker whose energy comes from his music. I joke often that Collin will live the longest in our family; he is such a pleasant guy to be around.

Naturally, the twins and Collin sought different career paths because they are wired differently. Understanding their natural bent is important for them as they navigate their careers.

I am a big proponent of personality profiles. Personality tests— which would have saved me the agony of taking engineering chemistry and calculus as a freshman—are a good exercise for learning how people are wired regardless of the stage of their career. We have a God-given wiring for how we see the world and interact with others. We aren't clones, and what motivates or encourages one person can discourage another.

One of the most popular personality assessments is the Myers-Briggs Type Indicator. Myers-Briggs looks at key categories, like whether a person is introverted or extroverted, a planner or someone who flies by the seat of their pants, and a thinker or a feeler. I am an extrovert, a planner, and a feeler. Myers-Briggs describes my decision-making this way:

[As a feeler,] I believe I can make the best decisions by weighing what people care about and the points-of-view of persons involved in a situation. I am concerned with values and what is the best for the people involved. I like to do whatever will establish or maintain harmony. In my relationships, I appear caring, warm, and tactful.[1]

I am the only "F" in our leadership group at JGR. The others are "Ts" (thinkers), which means they tend to be more analytical and less emotional in decision-making than I am. The stereotypical CEO profile is an introverted thinker.

The Enneagram is another great type profile that can be completed in fifteen minutes. The Enneagram has nine primary profiles, and I am a 3, or an "achiever."

CliftonStrengths, once known as StrengthsFinder, is another good test that evaluates a person's top five of thirty-four key traits. Mine are strategic, belief, responsibility, communication, and woo (meeting new people and "winning them over").

These profiles are helpful because they outline what motivates people and identify their strengths, weaknesses, and blind spots. The more employees who can take these tests and review them as a group or team, the better for the company, because they provide huge insights into getting the most out of everyone.

We gave a personality test to each member of our front office and placed everyone's results on a board for all to see. Managing employees became easier with the knowledge of what tactics they best respond to based on their personalities.

Every good organization needs people who complement each other's wiring, which means there's no one-size-fits-all vision for employees.

With J.D., Todd, and me, none of our profiles were even close to the same, and we perfectly complemented each other. Either Todd or J.D. balanced me in each of the areas where I struggled.

Todd is the most gifted person I have worked with from an operational standpoint. Todd has an almost photographic memory; he never took a single note during meetings. He could look at a department and, in his mind, reorganize it to be the most efficient operationally. He was excellent with people but could make tough decisions and promote or demote someone without becoming emotional. He eventually became our COO, and in many ways, he was the glue that held things together in our operation. Todd's role was 95 percent focused inside our building. My role was 95 percent *outside* our building, with sponsors, tracks, NASCAR, media, partners, and industry folks.

I am the type of person who sees the world three years from now. J.D. lived life in the here and now. Often, as I would stress about planning for a driver agreement that might be expiring in a year, J.D. would say, "I think it will all take care of itself" and direct me back to living in the moment. He didn't stress about the future.

Because I was the only feeler in the executive group, J.D. and Todd jokingly called me the "sensitive one." When we reached a decision, they would look to me and say something like, "Okay, Mr. Feeler. Are you okay with that?"

Every business issue and every life issue at some point comes down to people. Being an F reduces my sleep, but I believe my personality is one of the reasons God has me in this position. One of my missions in every meeting is to insert the people quotient, and my ability to place myself in others' situations has served me well through the years.

Whatever decision we are facing, I try to bring a compassionate perspective.

Let's say a driver is nearing the end of his career, and we need to make a decision to move forward with a different driver. That's a difficult, people-impacting decision. I'm thinking, *If I were that driver, how would I want to be told about this decision? How would I want to be treated?* That driver has become my friend, and disappointing a friend is difficult.

Since I'm a feeler, difficult people can drain me, because I take unfavorable comments personally. Negative body language by others is stressful for me. I hate harshness, and NASCAR is by its nature a harsh environment. I don't mean that as a knock; it's just that our sport is packed with highly competitive, type-A achievers.

Words of affirmation is my love language,[2] and as company president, I am in a position that does not bring much affirmation. I don't get my tires pumped often in this job. In fact, for someone who struggles with feelings of inadequacy and is self-conscious, it would be easy to spiral in this job because I could always do better. People can always be happier. When one of our cars wins a race, three teams leave the same track disappointed. I strive for work-life balance, but I know there is always another trip, another few hours of meetings, another dinner out with a customer that I could do to be better. How good is good enough?

I have learned to accept that God believed this would be a good place to prune me. My F side is an important component of our culture at JGR. We benefit from my ability to relate with people and feel alongside them. When someone has a tough decision to make, they'll ask me, "All right, Pern. What am I not thinking of?" Or "I'm giving you a heads-up on this. Is there anything I should think about before I do this?" Code word: "You're the sensitive one—how will this make other people feel?"

I take it as a privilege to be a voice of reason, as I like to describe my role. I'd like to think I have a good balance of leading with my heart and leading with my head. Our executive team needs an F just as much as it needs leaders who are not feelers. I fully recognize that if all the executives were Fs like me, we would probably go out of business. I mean, it would be a very pleasant environment, with all us feelers leading the company, but we would go bankrupt in a matter of months! But the team members we have complement each other well and lead our company with balance.

Understanding your own wiring and, as much as possible, the wiring of those you work with and for is important.

Along with understanding how you are wired, another way to add value to a company is by asking, "What am I good at?" and then finding ways to make your abilities known. It might mean starting a club or a committee or volunteering for something.

> Embracing your own gifts and wiring, rather than trying to be someone you are not, can add balance to your organization and set you apart.

When I asked myself early on what I was good at, I realized I loved being in front of people. I grew up wanting to be on TV. I went to J.D. with the idea that we could create a video for the company Christmas party. Think an episode of *Saturday Night Live* where we would make fun of ourselves and our drivers in a lighthearted way. The videos became a hit, and during the season, I would receive dozens of ideas from coworkers for the next Christmas party video. Even after Tony Stewart was no longer driving for us, he asked each year if he could make a cameo in the next video. Through the years, some of our drivers have appeared in the videos doing funny things that they probably wouldn't do for anything but a company Christmas video.

Am I still at JGR because of the Christmas videos? No, but the videos helped endear me to the drivers, made J.D. and me more relatable to employees, and added to the family culture at Joe Gibbs Racing.

## Be Great at the Little Things

Little things add up to big things.

Success and longevity begin by people determining to become great at the little things. I don't recall where I read this, but the secret to becoming an overnight sensation in the business world is to work at it every day over a long period of time. The journey to becoming company president usually consists of a series of promotions earned through thousands of little things done well enough that they eventually and systematically lead to the big things.

It's okay to dream about moving into a corner office right out of college, but don't expect to. The important question is, Are you willing to start in the broom closet and work your way into that corner office?

Coach won three Super Bowls. His first came at the end of the 1982 season. But to look into his first season as a coach, you have to go all the way back to 1964 at San Diego State University. His head coach was Don Coryell, now a member of the College Football Hall of Fame. The defensive coordinator on that staff was John Madden, who would earn enshrinement in the Pro Football Hall of Fame for his coaching accomplishments.

Coach Gibbs worked alongside these great coaches, and he received his opportunity because he offered to work for nothing. He likes to joke that his most important duty on that staff was picking up food for Coryell and Madden. That's how the three-time Super Bowl champion coach got his start: being willing to do the little things. And before he could hoist the Lombardi Trophy on national TV following a Super Bowl win, he first had to be great behind the scenes and, along the way, earn the trust of people who promoted him, step by step, responsibility by responsibility, into higher-profile positions.

In the earliest days of Joe Gibbs Racing, J.D., Todd, and I took on the mindset that no job was too small for us. I couldn't see how sitting around in the broom closet waiting on my next assignment was going to increase my value. Actually, I couldn't see much in the closet anyway with just the one lamp. The more visible and important opportunities that eventually came my way were the result of seeking out and excelling at mundane tasks.

I'm a decent writer, so early on that led me to drafting letters for front office people who weren't as good at writing. Admittedly, there were times when the mundane tasks seemed to be piling up and I battled the temptation to say, "I have better things to do today than write three paragraphs for you." But I didn't give in to that temptation.

Because I wrote the letters well and without complaining (aloud, anyway), I was eventually asked to write the team's press releases in the days before we had an in-house communications person. My work with the press releases led to one of our drivers asking me to help him write speeches for awards banquets and other big events. In NASCAR, drivers are the faces of the teams. In no other sport does one player carry such weight as the driver does for a race team. For that reason, a great deal of time and attention is spent on the relationship between the team and the driver. From the start, I wanted to build a relationship with each of our drivers and sought to serve and assist them in any way I could.

Writing those speeches built my relationships with the drivers, and that earned me their trust. Because of those relationships, people within the company came to me for help in resolving issues that involved drivers. I had worked my way into being an unofficial liaison for the drivers.

Back then, most drivers did not have agents. Joe recognized that because of my age, I related well to drivers as their peer, and he would ask me and usually J.D. to be part of conversations with the drivers when they discussed business opportunities and endorsements. Sometimes those talks occurred between just the driver and me.

If I had walked into JGR and said, "I want to be the guy that the drivers come to for help," I probably wouldn't have been around long enough to eventually take on that role. That's not how it works in the business world. But through letters, press releases, speeches, relationships, and gaining trust and credibility among JGR's key players, I made it there—and beyond.

Eventually. And it wasn't easy.

Occasionally I'll look back through my journals and come across entries expressing my frustration at seemingly not being noticed for the value I brought to our company.

> » *I'm being wasted here.*
> » *Lord, I'm not being utilized.*
> » *I'm not being challenged.*
> » *Will I be the T-shirt guy my entire life?*

I wrote those types of entries over the course of fifteen years. For all that time, I existed in this odd mix of being part of Coach's inner circle yet feeling unappreciated.

Even though I became an expert in licensing, my biggest value to Coach came as a part of his executive committee. I may have been in the middle of a licensing meeting only to be called into another meeting about switching crew chiefs or making a change in drivers. There were four people in the highest-level meetings: Coach, J.D., Todd, and me.

Coach trusted me. He respected the representation of the company I brought into those meetings. But no one else outside of that room knew the value I brought to JGR, and that bothered me. Mostly, it bothered my ego. For years, I carried a complex about being "the T-shirt guy" or being perceived as J.D.'s childhood buddy just along for the ride.

Coach knew my importance. Sometimes that was enough to satisfy me. After all, he was the guy who had entrusted Doug Williams and John Riggins with crucial roles with his Redskins teams. That same guy had picked me for a trusted role with his race team, and he was no dummy. Coach knew how to build teams that won big, and by bringing me into future-shaping decisions, he was trusting me.

But then there were other times when part of me—often a large part of me—wanted props for the influence I carried. I wanted others to know that I had been a part of landing a key sponsor, or that I had helped recruit a driver to JGR, or that what Coach shared in a meeting had come from me. I prayed for opportunities that would allow me to display my abilities and influence.

One of the challenges of delivering more than you cost to your company is that there will be an internal struggle with the fact that the personal payoff you are receiving from the company is less than you're delivering. You'll grow frustrated that you are underpaid and underappreciated. The juice sometimes doesn't seem worth the squeeze.

> Indispensable employees often feel underappreciated because their actual value exceeds their perceived value.

I experienced that. I considered whether I should leave JGR. I would tell myself that as long as I got after it and didn't sit at my desk and mope, then I would be rewarded with change. But the changes didn't come as quickly as I'd hoped. I had to stretch my patience to lengths I did not know my patience could stretch.

When I speak at universities, I share the advice to "bloom where you're planted." It's great to have aspirations for where you want to go, but getting there can sometimes mean thriving where you are now.

Today, as company president, I can see how my experiences—every high, every low, and everything in between—prepared me for this role. I have found myself able to relate to each department in the front office because, in one way or another, I worked at almost every job in the company. I wouldn't want to compare how I did those jobs then to those who perform them now, but I can at least understand their roles. I also understand the people filling those roles.

I am proof that doing small things pays off—and that the best way to become indispensable in any role is to deliver more value than you cost.

## TOPICS FOR REFLECTION

1. Delivering more than you cost means knowing yourself—your strengths, your weaknesses, your preferences, and where you can pitch in. Take several minutes and list some of your own traits. List at least five things that you think you're good at and five areas where you think you could improve. Then, if you feel comfortable, invite a trusted friend or a supervisor to make a similar list and review it with you. How can you lean more into your strengths, and in what ways can those around you help you in your weaknesses?

2. Delivering more than you cost can be discouraging at times, especially when you feel like your full worth isn't being recognized. Have you ever felt discouraged in this way? How did you react, and what was the result? If being trustworthy in little things leads to being entrusted with larger things, how can you keep your situation in perspective the next time you feel underappreciated?

# CREATE A WINNING CULTURE

## Chapter 5

# HONORING GOD FIRST AND FOREMOST

BEFORE *SECRET SAUCE* BECAME A PART of corporate speak, I remember the McDonald's commercials of the 1970s touting what made the Big Mac a Big Mac: "Two all-beef patties, special sauce, lettuce, cheese, pickles, onions, on a sesame-seed bun."

Now, companies self-evaluate to identify the secret sauce that gives their company its distinctive flavor or culture.

The recipe for a company's corporate culture—its secret sauce—is a mixture of corporate beliefs combined with how a company behaves, with the personality of its leader sprinkled in. The corporate culture, to change metaphors, is the engine that powers the company's mission. Every company has a corporate culture whether it attempts to forge one or not, and that culture, for better or worse, affects the company's performance toward its goals.

> Corporate culture = corporate beliefs +
> company behavior + leader's personality.

The Joe Gibbs Racing culture that enables us to fulfill our mission of going fast is summed up as a three-legged stool:

1. Honor God.
2. Put people before profits.
3. Relentlessly pursue winning.

To understand what the JGR culture looks like, it helps to understand our early years.

We started our team with more confidence than we should have had. We weren't arrogant; we simply didn't know what we didn't know. We were confident because of Coach's track record in football and the belief that his ability to evaluate, recruit, and assemble teams would translate well into NASCAR. Plus, hiring Jimmy Makar to run the team and Dale Jarrett as driver, even with Coach back in Washington with the Redskins, provided us a duo to follow that understood what it took to succeed in racing.

Not winning a race our first year was discouraging but not unexpected. To win the first race of our second season, the Daytona 500, was like injecting a big dose of "We're going to make it" into the company. We didn't win another race that year, but we finished top five thirteen times, and Dale placed fourth in the end-of-season driver standings.

Never did we believe our team was in jeopardy of not being able to stick around, but we did reach what has proved to be our lowest point in our third year, 1994.

We had just broken ground on a new building in late summer because our original building was not designed to house a race team. Securing a loan for the building was a huge step for Coach, who is conservative financially.

Soon after we broke ground, Dale informed us he would be leaving at the end of the season. He had accepted an offer from Yates Racing to fill the seat in the number 28 car after Ernie Irvan suffered life-threatening injuries. Dale's decision shocked us. His crew chief, Jimmy, was his brother-in-law. He also was still under contract to us. Although buying out a driver's contract wasn't out of the ordinary, our new team had not dealt with it and wasn't prepared for our driver to leave.

To top it all off, soon after Dale's announcement and for the first time in our short history, we missed a race when Dale failed to qualify for the October 2 race at North Wilkesboro Speedway in North Carolina. Of the forty-two cars competing for the thirty-six starting spots, we came in forty-first. I wasn't traveling to every race, and I was not in North Wilkesboro that day. I received a phone call informing me the team was coming home early. Imagine your favorite stick-and-ball team getting sent home without being able to participate in the game. I could feel the entire road crew's dejection in that phone call.

The next week was as down of a week as we had experienced. We debated whether breaking ground on a new home was wise when we didn't even have a driver for the next season. Coach seriously considered pulling out of the property deal.

But there's always another race, and next on the schedule was Charlotte Motor Speedway, which we and most other NASCAR teams consider our home track. Dale took his first lead of the day with four laps to go and was stretching his lead when a crash brought out the caution flag on the next-to-last lap. Dale took the victory under the yellow flag. A week after not qualifying for a race, we were celebrating in Victory Lane.

"Are you sure you want to leave?" Jimmy jokingly asked Dale.

(Two interesting notes from the win: First, Dale was wearing the Dallas Cowboys helmet again in that race. Second, the car Dale passed to take the lead was Yates Racing's number 28, the car he would drive the next season, which Kenny Wallace was driving on a fill-in basis.)

With three races remaining on the schedule, winning in Charlotte infused our team with confidence that we could carry into the off-season. We continued with plans for building our new home.

Then Coach recruited a soon-to-be winner to fill the seat in our Interstate Batteries car: Bobby Labonte, a young, competitive, aggressive Texan who had finished as runner-up behind Jeff Gordon for Rookie of the Year in 1993. Bobby had placed top five only once in his sixty-three races, but we could sense that with Jimmy's guidance, Bobby was ready to win.

Bobby placed second in two of the 1995 season's first four races and then notched his first career victory in the eleventh stop on the schedule, the Coca-Cola 600 in Charlotte. He won two more races that season. Bobby clearly was even better than we'd expected, and he made us a legitimate contender week in and week out. Bobby kept improving as a driver, and in 1999 he finished second in the points race. The following year, he led the points standings for twenty-five consecutive races on his way to a runaway Cup Series championship.

When Bobby's eleven-year run with us ended in 2005, he had won twenty-one races and almost $45 million in prize money with JGR. That was enough to later earn him induction into the NASCAR Hall of Fame alongside Coach and Tony Stewart.

In Joe Gibbs Racing history, Bobby is the driver who took us from our lowest valley to the top of the mountain.

Our mission statement at Joe Gibbs Racing says, "Our goal is to win races and championships for our partners and to see in our results things that would not have been possible except with the direct intervention of God."

The Dale/Bobby transition was Exhibit A for our mission statement.

## An Upsetting Ride with Tony Stewart

A seminal moment that changed the trajectory of our company came in 1997, when after two good seasons with Bobby in our number 18 car, we reached the decision that in order to become a better race team, we needed to add a second car. With one team, one sponsor, and one portion of race winnings, we had maxed out every efficiency we could find as a single team. To compete with the larger teams, we needed more people and more equipment.

Adding a second team would provide us with the scale to create redundancies in personnel, equipment, and expenses within the two teams. Additional sponsorship money could be turned into the engineers and equipment we lacked to compete at the top level.

At that time, most of the organizations that fielded multiple cars tended to field an A team and a B team, with obvious differences in how well each team ran.

"We're going to do this differently than everyone's done this," Coach adamantly stated. "I do not want an A team and a B team. I want two A teams." I heard him say at least a hundred times, "Two A teams or we aren't doing it."

Being a great team builder, Coach chose to have the current driver and crew chief help pick the new driver and crew chief. That way they could never come to Coach and say, "I can't work with these people" without Coach responding, "Well, you picked them." Plus, Jimmy had built our first team as crew chief. Why wouldn't he be part of building the second team?

Coach also decided to give our employees—especially those directly tied to our first car—stake in the second team.

"We're going to give everyone in the shop a bonus on both cars," he told us. "It won't be us versus them. It will be if one wins, we all win, including the crew chiefs."

He also said that both teams would be housed in the same building. Other NASCAR organizations with multiple cars usually separated their teams into different buildings. With our two teams working right on top of each other every day, they would have to work together. I figured Coach's move would either prove brilliant or fail miserably. Regardless, we would find out!

Bobby and Jimmy were part of our meeting to discuss potential drivers. We all had been assigned to bring a list of drivers we should consider, even if the drivers were not currently racing in NASCAR. Each of us wrote names on a piece of paper and placed our papers in a hat. One by one, lists were pulled from the hat and the names read aloud. Tony Stewart was the only driver whose name appeared on everyone's lists.

"Who is this Tony Stewart?" Coach asked us.

"He's the Indy Racing League champion," I answered. "He's won in everything he's ever raced."

Tony had started driving competitively at age seven in go-kart races. He had worked his way up through various levels of motorsports, with tremendous success at dirt tracks, to compete in open-wheel racing. He ultimately won the 1996–97 IRL championship. Tony had given stock car racing a try by driving in a limited number of events in the Busch (now Xfinity) Series the previous two years.

I remember one of us saying, "We're never going to get him, but we should go talk to him."

Chevy was our manufacturer at the time, and when Coach asked his Chevy contacts for an opinion on Tony, he was told, "He's phenomenal, but good luck getting him." The more Coach looked into Tony, the more determined he became to build our second team around him.

Coach is not just an amazing recruiter; he is also an obsessive one. I have joked that the secret behind Coach's ability to land sponsors and drivers is that he keeps calling them until they finally concede, "Fine, we'll do it. Please, just stop calling me."

Coach talked to anyone he could find who knew Tony, but he was having trouble making contact with Tony himself. So he obtained Tony's mom's phone number. And then Tony's girlfriend's number. Finally, Coach was able to set up a meeting with Tony in his hometown of Indianapolis. Coach asked J.D. and me to accompany him and Don Meredith to Indiana. J.D. and I were close in age to Tony, and Coach thought our presence might make Tony more comfortable.

We met Tony at a Steak 'n Shake near Indianapolis Motor Speedway. Joe had been out of coaching for five years, but he remained in the public spotlight through his work as an analyst on NBC's NFL pregame show. We were sitting in a booth with Tony in his hometown, and at least ten people approached us and asked for Coach's autograph without acknowledging Tony.

"Man, you're a pretty big deal," Tony said to Coach, who, of course, deflected the comment.

The Steak 'n Shake meal and conversation went well enough for Coach and Don to leave to meet with Tony's business manager.

"Go entertain Tony while we meet with his manager," Coach told J.D. and me before leaving the restaurant.

Tony offered to show us around Indianapolis. His car was a two-seater. Obviously, on a business trip for Joe Gibbs Racing, the guy named Gibbs was going to get the passenger seat. So yours truly, the gofer, crawled into the hatch area, and Tony took us to see his home and other places that were important to him. Let's just say that off the track, race car drivers don't drive like a grandma on her way to church. We were flying around corners, and I was in the back, with no seat belt, getting rolled around. And, by the way, I've always had major motion sickness issues. I was holding my lips together to keep from throwing up in the back of Tony's car.

*Um, sorry, Coach,* I could imagine myself saying, *but I'm not sure Tony's going to want to join us after I puked all over his car.*

Tony had signed to race part-time with another NASCAR team in a lower series. Because that team couldn't offer Tony the opportunity to run full-time, we were able to buy out Tony's contract for $500,000. I'll never forget that owner, before taking the check from Coach, giving him one more chance to back out, asking, "Are you *sure* you want to do this?"

Coach was sure.

The owner's caution came from Tony's reputation for being a fiery competitor and an emotional guy with a temper. That turned out to be true! Tony raced because he loved racing and wanted nothing less than a victory from every race.

Tony was an elite talent. But when we signed him, he impressed us most with his maturity by telling Coach that he wanted to start out in the minor series because he didn't believe he was ready to run at the Cup level. Even though Tony had limited stock-car experience, he could have stepped into the Cup series as a better driver than half the field he would have faced each weekend. He didn't want to just *race* at the Cup level, though. He wanted to *win*. In his mind, the best route for accomplishing his goal was to spend a year gaining more stock-car experience in the lower series.

In 1998, we ran Tony in twenty-two Busch Series races. Although he didn't win any, he held the lead in six races. He also wrecked out of six races. Tony could be all over the place at times during that first season with us, but he also showed flashes of the brilliance that would come during his Cup career.

In preparation for the 1999 Cup season, we visited a company that had agreed to sponsor Tony. At the meeting to finalize the deal, we were told the company had decided to go in a different direction. Coach got angrier than I have ever seen him in a sponsorship meeting. He has this way of pointing his finger at someone to emphasize what he's saying, and he stood up, pointed his finger at the guy who had backed out of the agreement, and said, "Mark my words: you will go down as the man who let Tony Stewart go."

In need of a sponsor, we traveled to Atlanta to meet with Home Depot and its cofounder, Arthur Blank. Home Depot's competitor, Lowe's, was already in NASCAR. Arthur said the number one thing employees would tell him when he visited stores was "We need to be in NASCAR."

Arthur envisioned a NASCAR team rallying his employees together around the country every Sunday afternoon. The company was involved in most pro sports, but employees rooted for teams in their regions. Employees in Seattle, for example, had different favorite teams than those in Dallas or Miami. NASCAR would act as sort of an alma mater to unify all of Arthur's employees on Sundays. Just like when someone at an airport gives a nod or says, "Go Heels" (or whatever the appropriate team is) to someone else wearing a shirt from their alma mater, NASCAR would serve that role for Home Depot employees.

Home Depot signed on and enjoyed more than a decade-long run with Tony that delivered more than we had hoped. In the process, NASCAR became part of Home Depot's culture.

After Bob Nardelli became CEO in 2000, he hosted Tony's entire number 20 team at his home twice a year for the races in Atlanta. On our first visit to Bob's home, J.D. and I were receiving a tour when we heard someone downstairs playing the piano and singing. As we moved closer to the music, J.D. said of the singer, "Dang, he's pretty good."

"Yeah," I said. "He sounds almost like Kenny Rogers."

When we walked down the stairs and the piano came into view, J.D. exclaimed, "It *is* Kenny Rogers! Man, you don't see that every day!"

Kenny Rogers was one of Bob's neighbors.

Bob, like Arthur, was a huge advocate of our team and recognized the value our partnership provided Home Depot, its associates, and its brand. Both men remain good friends of ours at JGR.

## Completing the Climb to the Top

Coach's "two cars, one team" approach to expansion worked instantly. In our first seven seasons as a one-car team, we won nine races, and the highest that one of our drivers finished in the season points race was Dale Jarrett's fourth-place finish in our second year. In 1999, our first season with two cars, we won eight races and finished as runner-up eight times. Tony and Bobby placed first and second in a race twice. In the Drivers' Championship, Bobby finished second and Tony came in fourth.

Coach's idea to have Bobby and Jimmy play a role in selecting the second driver and crew chief set the tone from the outset. Before 1999, our competition meetings included one crew chief and one driver talking about how their car was handling. When we added the second car, our competition meetings included both drivers and both crew chiefs. They compared notes and shared how their cars responded to various adjustments. One crew chief could then say, "We're going to try this. You try that, and we'll find out which one works best."

Different drivers tend to perform better at certain types of tracks. It made sense to position the drivers to learn from each other's strengths. Bobby and Tony made each other better. They had different backgrounds—Bobby came up in stock cars, Tony in open wheel. They liked their cars set up differently, but they invariably helped each other. This is still the case at JGR, with four drivers together in competition meetings. Denny Hamlin is a master of short tracks and might be the best Martinsville Speedway driver ever. Kyle Busch had struggled at short tracks. Kyle learned from Denny and became a better short-track driver and, ultimately, a more complete driver. Kyle has helped Denny improve at the mile-and-a-half tracks. They both have become better drivers because they work together, and the benefits to our team are evident.

> In a winning culture, members are intentional about making each other better.

From the start of our expansion to two teams, our drivers not only helped each other improve by working together off the track, but the on-track measuring stick served as an instant spark. Sports are built on competition, and it doesn't matter whether you're competing against a brother or a best friend; you want to win. Consider the NFL, for example, and the difference when a quarterback goes into training camp with no competition for his starting position compared with a team that has two first-round picks at quarterback who are competing every day of camp for the starting job. There is no room for complacency with competition. In our sport, drivers from the same team will help each other on the track to some degree. But in the end, it's pretty much every driver for himself, and as someone who sees the drivers climb out of their cars after races, I can attest that the only thing a driver hates more than losing is losing to a teammate.

The same principle applied to crew chiefs, engineers, and on down the line. Each week became a friendly competition for who could beat whom. Two cars, one team resulted in two cars pushing each other to greatness.

Again, all credit to Coach for establishing the tone and creating financial incentives for everyone in our team when one of our cars won. Crew members on Bobby's car had reason to work during the week with crew members on Tony's car. They could have taken an attitude of *We're the original car here. They're the second team, and the company's attention needs to be focused on us winning.* But Coach didn't create a culture that allowed for selfishness, and as we grew, he didn't allow that to creep into the building. He expanded us in a way that we remained a true team. When Tony's car won, everyone in the building—and that included Bobby's guys—earned a bonus. The bonus was not as much as if their own car had won, because we didn't want the team that hadn't won to be as excited as the winning team. But Coach did want to demonstrate that we recognized they had played a role in Tony's victory.

Coach's plan worked. In our second season as a two-car team, Bobby brought Joe Gibbs Racing its first championship. Two years later, in 2002, Tony won the championship. The way we added a second car elevated us into a legitimate championship-caliber team.

One of my fondest memories from working at JGR is the celebration banquet for Bobby's 2000 championship. NASCAR's season-ending awards banquet was at the Waldorf Astoria in New York City. My wife and I sat at a table that included J.D. and his wife, Melissa; Todd and Sara Meredith; and Don and Sally Meredith. I remember looking around the room and seeing racing icons Roger Penske, Rick Hendrick, and Jack Roush, and thinking, *We just won the championship!*

I flashed back through memories of us landing Dale Jarrett as the driver to help establish our team. And then how he left and we hired a young Bobby Labonte, who had never won a race, days after we almost called off building our new home. And now Bobby was the man of the night as NASCAR's top driver.

Norm Miller of Interstate Batteries, our first sponsor, gave the acceptance speech on behalf of the sponsor. Typical Norm, he almost got the hook off the stage because he spent nearly all his allotted ten minutes sharing about his faith on national TV. Norm and his brother Tommy were the guys who took a chance on our team when Coach had nothing but that dream on a sheet of paper. As far as I was concerned, they should have allowed Norm to talk as long as he wanted! I have so much respect for Norm, not only because he had the guts to make the decision to partner with us but also because he uses his platform to share his faith boldly, give generously, and run a company guided by strong conviction and selfless leadership.

To have ascended to the top of our sport was another clear example of God's faithfulness to our team. No matter how many championships we wind up winning, I will never forget celebrating that first one in New York City. Throughout the night, I felt a sense of God saying, "I've got you." I never want our culture to become one in which I no longer have that sense.

We seek to honor God in all facets of our business, but the foundation of our "honor God" culture is our leader's faith and how he incorporates prayer into his leadership. From our start—and this continues today—Coach has led a Monday-morning prayer meeting for a small group of us. In the early days, we prayed for employees by name. Now that we've grown, we pray for departments and our sponsors. We have started every workweek for almost three decades by thanking the Lord and, often, pleading with him for wisdom and intervention in whatever crisis looms ahead.

Perhaps my best memories of Joe Gibbs Racing will be of our small group huddling around Coach's table and praying every Monday morning. Although our desire to honor God goes mostly unseen in our performance on the track, this is the beating heart of our company and our winning culture. We wouldn't be Joe Gibbs Racing without it.

## TOPICS FOR REFLECTION

1. I've said that the recipe for corporate culture is a mix of corporate beliefs, company behavior, and the leader's personality. At Joe Gibbs Racing, that has included our priorities to honor God, put people above profits, and relentlessly pursue winning.

   » How would you describe the corporate culture where you work?

   » What values does your organization subscribe to, and how are those values borne out in the decisions that are made?

   » What are the key traits of your organization's leaders?

   » How does your organization's culture affect your day-to-day job and decision-making?

   » Ask yourself, "How can I positively affect and reflect our corporate culture today?"

2. One way that we have relentlessly pursued winning at JGR is by leaning on each other's strengths and by helping each other get better.

   » What key strengths do you contribute to your team?

   » In what areas do you think you could use your strengths to help your teammates get better?

   » In what ways can you rely on your teammates' strengths to bring better results?

## Chapter 6

# FROM FAMILY BUSINESS TO FACTORY

In January 2004, on our first day back in the office after the Christmas and New Year's break, Coach and J.D. walked into my office and shut the door—a sure indication something big was happening. The sheepish looks on their faces seconded the motion.

Coach sat down and looked at me before asking, "What do you think about what's going on with the Redskins right now?"

Coach and J.D. knew I was as big a Redskins fan as there was. I immediately stood.

"What are you asking me?!"

I expected Coach to tell me he was buying the Redskins.

"What would you think about me going back to help them get things fixed?" he asked.

"You mean, like being their coach?" I asked.

"Yeah. Maybe."

"That's the greatest thing I've ever heard!" I exclaimed. The Redskins had made the playoffs only once in the eleven seasons since Coach had retired.

"Really?" Coach asked. "You're not worried about the race team?"

"Heck no," I replied. "We've just signed a bunch of long-term sponsorships. We have our drivers locked in. We're in great shape for the season. Don't worry about us. Go rescue the Redskins!"

Because I was sworn to secrecy until the official announcement, the next two days were excruciating. Holding on to news as top secret as Coach returning to Washington gave me a glimpse of what my dad's career in the CIA must have felt like.

Coach wanted to tell our drivers, Bobby and Tony, the news face-to-face before they heard through the media, so he headed to Daytona, where they were testing. He flew in on the Redskins' private plane with a giant Redskins helmet painted on the side. When he met Tony at the airport, Tony said, "Well, I kind of figured out why you're here based on the Redskins plane that's parked right next to mine."

Coach's four seasons back in Washington are among the fondest memories of my career. Joe Gibbs Racing bought a suite at FedEx Field, and most Sundays in the fall, instead of going to the race, I would host JGR sponsors in the suite. My young sons often went with me. Before each game, we took our twenty or so guests down to the sidelines. After games, Coach came up to the box to greet everyone.

Coach going back to the Redskins produced another valuable lesson in the traits of the greats I have been around. Coach was not afraid of failure. He jumped right back into coaching despite how his wife, Pat, responded when he asked her about returning to football: "You're going to ruin your good name." Coach had nothing to prove. He already was in the Hall of Fame, yet he possessed passion and vision for what could be in Washington. Great leaders should take risks—and listen to their wives.

> Great leaders are not afraid of taking risks,
> even when they have nothing to prove.

## Delivering for FedEx

When Joe returned to coaching, we decided to expand again by adding a third team. The same principle from our first expansion remained in place: three cars, one team, with our drivers and crew chiefs included in the expansion decisions.

Adding a third car signified a major shift because we added a hundred employees, transitioning us from a family business into a racing factory. The entire feel of the company changed.

Because our sport begins and ends with sponsorship, we needed a partner to make a third car possible. We headed to Memphis, Tennessee, home of FedEx. FedEx's main competitor—the brown one—already was involved in racing, and FedEx was looking at getting into the sport.

Fred Smith, FedEx founder and CEO, also owned part of the Washington Redskins, and Redskins owner Dan Snyder provided intel on his experience negotiating with FedEx.

"One of the guys you're going to have to convince is a guy I've nicknamed 'Mr. No,'" Mr. Snyder said.

"Mr. No" was Mike Glenn, and Mr. Snyder told us we could expect about twenty FedEx executives to meet with us in their boardroom. Mr. Smith would sit at the head of the table. The highest-ranking execs typically sat closest to the CEO, and Mike would be seated next to Mr. Smith.

"Mike's a great guy," Mr. Snyder said. "But he's going to ask all the difficult questions, and know that he's a guy you have to get through, because he says no to everything."

We spent two months preparing our presentation. Our PowerPoint covered seventy-five pages. We hadn't planned on going through all seventy-five, but we had all our bases covered so nothing would catch us off guard. We took visuals with us, including die-cast cars with the FedEx logo.

As the vice president of marketing, I flew to Memphis with Coach, J.D., and Dean Noble, who would oversee the sponsorship if it came to be. We encountered a mix-up on the rental car. If only we had been aligned with Toyota at that time! All we could rent was a Dodge Neon, which looked to be the size of a go-kart. Not only was the car bright red, but "Neon" was emblazoned in bright purple on the back.

*Boy*, I thought, *FedEx is going to be really impressed with us.*

Embarrassed by the car, we parked far away from the entrance to FedEx's headquarters, and the four of us suit-wearing, NASCAR executives seeking a major sponsorship worth seven figures walked almost the length of the parking lot in the Memphis heat. Trust me—that scene looked less ridiculous than the rental car.

We entered the boardroom, and Mr. Smith was indeed seated at the head of the table. He was a celebrity in the business world because of FedEx's success, even making a cameo appearance in the movie *Cast Away*. I quickly surveyed the rest of the executives around the table, and my gut told me that none of them had attended a NASCAR race. They were gracious as they met us, but I sensed they were around the table because Mr. Smith had told them to attend our meeting.

*Man*, I thought, *I don't want to waste these people's time. I think they belong in racing, but we have to do a good job of telling our story.*

Fortunately, we were prepared. We had rehearsed our presentation for the past month. We knew exactly what we were going to say, who was going to say it, and when. As we were setting out our visuals, I pulled out a poster-sized EA Sports game with Tony Stewart on the cover. I knew the Home Depot uniform Tony was wearing would be an eye-catcher to a company looking to expand its brand into a new market.

"Hey," Mr. Smith said, "if we get into NASCAR, can you promise us we'll get on the cover of one of those games?"

Coach looked at me. "Dave, why don't you talk to them about merchandising and how that works?"

That was page forty of the presentation. We hadn't even started the first page yet!

"Sure, I'd love to," I said, scrambling through my PowerPoint slides. We rearranged our entire pitch on the fly.

Afterward, we walked back to the rental car, which was easy to find because it stood out in the parking lot. I felt like our presentation had been all over the place.

"I don't know how this is going to turn out," I told the others.

Seventeen years later, I'd say it has turned out well.

Before FedEx signed on with us, it had never paid to place its logo on an athlete. There was the FedEx Orange Bowl college football game, the FedExForum arena in Memphis, and FedExField. Soon after FedEx partnered with us, the PGA Tour named its playoffs the FedExCup. FedEx attached its name to arenas and events, not to people.

FedEx was the best at hosting sporting events. Bringing customers to events allowed them not only to say thank you but to spend valuable time building relationships. Entering NASCAR would provide FedEx with thirty-six opportunities to host people in key markets around the country where the company wanted to grow its business.

So, for the first time, FedEx chose to have an individual athlete represent the company.

Unfortunately, FedEx's first season with us didn't get off to a great start. The number 11 car crashed out of the Daytona 500 and blew an engine in the second race. In May, that car failed to qualify for the Coca-Cola 600 in Charlotte, and we worked out a deal for that race to switch FedEx over to Bobby Labonte's number 18 car sponsored by Interstate Batteries. Bobby led late before being nosed out by Jimmie Johnson for the checkered flag by a margin of less than half a car length.

Heading into the final seven races of the season, that was one of only two top-ten finishes for FedEx, and it didn't even come in its own car.

We made a driver change midseason, bringing up Denny Hamlin from the Busch Series—NASCAR's equivalent of the minor leagues—to make his Cup Series debut. Denny gave FedEx three top-ten finishes over the final two months and started the next-to-last race from the pole position. Denny and FedEx have been paired ever since and have won the Daytona 500 three times.

Denny's relationship with FedEx illustrates how there is much more to being a driver than what takes place behind the steering wheel. Because Denny would represent FedEx, he traveled to Memphis to be schooled as though he were becoming a FedEx salesperson. He learned how to talk FedEx's language to the point that when someone would ask Denny to talk about FedEx's relationship with, for example, St. Jude Children's Research Hospital, Denny could answer like a FedEx salesperson. In essence, he *became* a FedEx salesperson.

Our partnership with FedEx reflects the changing nature of sponsorships. Winning races and leading laps are important for FedEx. Winning is an expectation. But sponsorship now also requires a deliverable. FedEx entered NASCAR with a well-researched and clear objective: persuading more people in Middle America—such as small business owners—to ship through FedEx.

FedEx's tangible return on investment from NASCAR is shipping. FedEx is the perfect example of a business-to-business company because virtually every company in the world ships through someone, and we came to recognize that FedEx's customer base is every company we do business with.

The key deliverable we provide FedEx is more shipping business.

Coach has ended up becoming one of FedEx's best salesmen. It almost has become a game for us, guessing how long it will take in a meeting with any new partner before Coach asks, "Who do you do your shipping with?" (Usually within the first ten minutes.) Coach will then move in on closing the sale by asking, "What if we could get you a discount on that $10 million, $20 million, $30 million you spend a year by switching over to FedEx?"

Coach was so good at recruiting new business for FedEx that before long, about $300 million a year worth of business had been switched to FedEx as a result of our relationship. Now, we have an employee whose chief job is to pitch FedEx to all our partners. That kind of measurable return is why FedEx has remained in the sport for so long. We know we have to earn our keep by bringing them measurable business.

> **Having tangible, measurable deliverables is the only way to know if you are winning or losing.**

The JGR-FedEx association is one of the great partnerships in sports. And Mr. No? Mike Glenn became one of our greatest advocates. Even though he has retired from FedEx, he sits on our advisory board, and he is a huge proponent of our racing program. He is one of the wisest business minds I have worked with, plus a great friend.

FedEx coming on board was a huge step for us to move up another rung in the NASCAR team hierarchy. But adding that third team posed cultural challenges: How would we maintain our culture with such a tectonic shift in the environment? How would we remain a people-first, family business that was transitioning into more of a factory?

We tackled the first question by relentlessly pursuing winning. The scale we now possessed made us instantly better, because we didn't have to hire or buy one of everything for the third car. The shift to specialization that began with bringing on our second team was completed by the addition of our third team. For example, the work of an engineer performing research and development that made two cars go fast could make three cars go fast. The same number of people who designed chassis for two cars could build chassis for three cars. The dynamometer that tested the suspension on two cars could test three.

Scaling brought us the freedom to create a list of areas where we were able to create new, more specialized positions—like a carbon fiber department with employees focused on building lighter and stronger parts for all our cars. Specialization led to more people working horizontally across departments instead of vertically within one car's team.

The dividends were clear on the track. In our first season as a three-car team, Tony won our third championship—a gratifying title for us with Joe coaching in the NFL again.

At the postseason awards banquet in New York, Coach attended along with Dan Snyder. But J.D. stood on the platform and delivered the owner's speech as the head of a championship team, which was extra special for me because that moment symbolized that J.D. had arrived. We were no longer college kids. I could not have been prouder of my friend.

## The View from the White House

That championship earned us an invitation from President George W. Bush to visit the White House the following January. Growing up in DC and knowing my dad had been to the White House in his role at the CIA made the day surreal. I remember looking out toward Pennsylvania Avenue and recalling all the times I had driven by the White House growing up. The perspective looking out *from* the White House instead of in *toward* our president's home was amazing.

Tony's number 20 car was parked close to the White House and stanchioned off. We were told that Coach and Tony would go into the Oval Office to meet with the president. The other thirty of us stood near Tony's car in the freezing weather, but we were all so pumped to be at the White House that the temperature didn't matter.

Soon, out came Coach and Tony with President Bush to look at the car. The president spotted us and asked, "Who are these guys?"

"That's my crew," Tony answered.

"Well, why are they standing there?" the president asked in his down-home Texas style. "You guys come on!"

In a millisecond, all thirty of us jumped over the stanchions and swarmed the president. The Secret Service agents started touching the small radios in their ears and talking to one another. They must have briefly lost sight of the president in the crowd we created around him.

President Bush was awesome. He chatted with us and started shaking everyone's hand. Jason Shapiro was our unofficial crew comedian. When the president turned to him, Jason said, "It's nice to meet you, sir. I'd like to welcome you to the family. Um . . . we have a tradition among the pit crew, and it's something we do to everybody before every race."

"What's that?" the president asked.

Jason reached around the president, patted him on the butt twice, and said, "Good game!"

Without missing a beat, the president turned to one of the women on our staff and said, "I'm glad he didn't do that to you!"

I have a good friend who works for the Secret Service. When he and I talked later about our team's visit, he told me that when Jason patted the president's butt, word came through the Secret Service agents' earpieces that "Number One has been touched. Repeat, Number One has been touched." Jason was lucky he didn't get taken out!

As I waited for my turn with the president—to shake his hand, not to pat his backside—I came up with my line for greeting him: "I want you to know that my father worked for your father." Just as I reached out to shake the president's hand, I noticed the white pinstripes on his navy suit had "George W. Bush" in a tiny step-and-repeat pattern.

Those little letters sewn into his stripes were the coolest thing I had ever seen. All I could do was point to the stripes and say, "Now *that* is awesome!"

The president gave me his classic smirk. "Hey, it's good to be the president."

I did manage to tell the president about my dad working at the CIA when George H. W. Bush was its director, and he told me, "Thank your father for his service for me."

President Bush spent about forty-five minutes with us, and he made us feel like we were buddies hanging out. When the time came for him to leave for his next appointment, he stated loudly, "Man! You guys are fun! Unfortunately, I've got to leave to go meet with the ambassador from Turkey who's waiting in my office."

Before I left the White House grounds, I took another moment to reflect on how I was standing at the most famous address in the world because of a job that started in a broom closet.

It would be 2015 before I visited the White House again, after Kyle Busch secured the championship and a trip to visit President Barack Obama. We were welcomed into the White House and allowed to roam even more than the previous time. I found President Obama to be as warm and engaging as President Bush. And nobody patted his butt!

On this visit, the team was introduced in the press briefing room, and I was introduced by the president of the United States as the president of Joe Gibbs Racing. Wow! A US president introducing me by name at the White House—not bad for the T-shirt guy.

Receiving an invitation to the White House is a great honor. I don't care who is holding office or about any of the politics involved in a visit. If I'm invited to the White House, I'm going. I have always wondered why someone would turn down a personal meeting with the president. When else will you get a one-on-one chance to say what's on your mind? I could have shared any number of things with Presidents Bush and Obama during my few moments with them. I chose to shake their hands and thank them for recognizing our team and for doing what they believed was best for our country. And I would say that to any president, even if I disagreed about what that looks like. We are all Americans.

Interestingly, Kyle's 2015 championship coincided with yet another expansion. We added our fourth car that season, again including the existing teams as part of the process and creating financial bonuses for all employees. We won a then-NASCAR record fourteen of the thirty-six races that year, and Kyle took the season points championship despite missing eleven races because of a bad wreck at Daytona. Each expansion has led almost immediately to a championship.

But while our culture of winning grew along with our company's size, the challenge of keeping an employee-first culture grew as well. We had transformed from a small family business to a racing factory and, finally, to a company bursting at the seams.

## TOPICS FOR REFLECTION

1. Great leaders are not afraid of taking risks. It was risky for Coach to return to the Redskins when his reputation was already secure, especially when his race team was expanding.

   » When you make tough decisions, what criteria do you use for evaluation?

   » How would you rate your risk tolerance on a scale of 1 to 10?

2. Measurable expectations are very important so that we always know if we are winning or losing. In landing FedEx as a sponsor, delivering more shipping business was the measurable goal.

   » Who is your customer, and do you have clearly defined expectations with them?

   » How about you personally? When you go in to work each day, do you have measurable goals and expectations? How about anyone who works for you?

## Chapter 7

# FITTING THE JOE MOLD

WHEN I REFLECT ON THE EARLY DAYS of our company, the family feel stands out most. We came into NASCAR as a small, one-car team, and we embraced our underdog role. Competing against bigger teams like Hendrick and Roush made for a difficult task. But we accepted the challenge, and we had fun competing.

The age of specialization had not yet arrived in NASCAR, especially for the smaller teams, so everyone on our team had to work like a utility player. Jimmy, the crew chief, also served as jackman on race days, hauling the jack around to each side of the car and lifting the car for the tire changers during pit stops. That's unheard of today for a crew chief, who sits atop the pit box during a race and leads the team like a head coach.

J.D. was a catchall, and in our second season, he joined the pit crew as a tire changer. Mechanics' duties weren't divided up by specialties, with all mechanics working on any area of the car that needed attention. Initially, I did not travel to every race, but the rest of the team went to the track each week. We drove together to races that were within six hours, which accounted for most of our schedule. There were only a few restaurants near our office, and during the week we ate lunch together almost every day.

Because we spent so much time together at home and on the road, we were a close-knit team.

Despite the challenges of being a small team with big goals, the atmosphere in our building was usually lighthearted. We worked hard and had fun.

We waged an ongoing war around the building of knocking food out of people's hands. If someone walked by J.D. or me holding a sandwich or an ice cream cone without a firm grip—wham!—it was on the floor.

The mechanics called us front-office workers "carpet walkers," and they played pranks on us that were an odd combination of ruthless and kindhearted.

Once, I placed a newspaper ad to sell my car. Someone responded to the ad, and I arranged to show the car at our office. The mechanics found out and poured transmission fluid into my engine. When the prospective buyer took the car for a test drive, smoke poured out of the hood like a rock concert. The prospective buyer ended the test drive quickly, much to the delight of our onlooking mechanics.

Another time, the mechanics put tie wraps around my drive shaft so that when the drive shaft spun, the wraps clicked. It took me a week to figure out the source of the clicking. They also habitually made fun of my closet/office by posting signs on the door that read, "Caution: People inside" and "Do not feed the animal."

Numerous pranks revolved around fish, starting at a test session on a hot day at Talladega Superspeedway. Some of the guys bought a big mackerel and duct-taped it underneath the hood of a rental car. The fish smell drifted through the car's interior vents, and no one could figure out where the smell was coming from. That led to a fish being taped underneath our parts guy's desk after he left the office on a Friday afternoon. By Monday morning, the entire shop reeked of dead fish. The parts guy retaliated by packing dead fish in a box and sending the box to someone in our office.

One of the guys kept a horn shaped like a French horn in his toolbox. He would fill the horn with baby powder and talk someone into playing it. Because of the instrument's shape, when that person blew through the mouthpiece, the baby powder flew all over them.

A long-running prank was one of my favorites, even though I once fell victim to it. One of our mechanics invented a mythical car part called a long weight. When a rookie joined us and he seemed primed to fall for the prank, a mechanic would rush up to him in a panic at a racetrack and say, "Hey, we're in a real bind! Can you run through the garage and find me a long weight?" Then the rookie would hurry over to another team's trailers and ask for a long weight, only to be told something like, "We're using ours, but go over to that trailer and ask them." This game of pass-the-rookie continued until he finally caught on.

I miss those days. We had to watch our backs and hold tight to our food in hallways, but the pranks endeared team members to one another. Pranks were part of building a family atmosphere into our culture. Maintaining that part of our culture has proved to be the hardest part of our growth.

## Finding "Butt-Busters"

Culture starts at the top of a company. Good leaders surround themselves with good people. No great coach has won without great players.

Any good business leader will tell you they need to be surrounded by great people who fit their mold in order to achieve their mission. Coach has a set mold he looks for in potential employees.

In many ways, Coach's presence gives us an unfair advantage. When it comes to business, racing is all he thinks about because racing, unlike most of our competitors, is his only business. He wakes up and goes to bed thinking about racing.

More important, Coach understands people, understands how to motivate them to work together toward a goal, and understands team dynamics. As he proved with the Redskins before creating our team, he knows how to build and lead winning teams.

But culture only *starts* at the top; it must be nurtured throughout the company at every level.

> Culture may start at the top,
> but it must be nurtured at every level of the company.

When Coach started our company, he knew he wasn't a car guy. After hiring Dale Jarrett and Jimmy Makar, he turned over finding the rest of the team members to Jimmy, besides the three musketeers, of course. Coach's reputation as a winner in the NFL resulted in a solid pool of experienced candidates wanting to be a part of establishing his new team. Coach didn't need to understand the nuts and bolts of building a NASCAR team, because Jimmy did. Coach only needed to rely on his ability to understand people.

I witnessed Coach build a winning culture, and now I am charged with maintaining that culture. I know the difficulties of both. Over its near-thirty-year history, JGR has evolved from a company with one car to four, eighteen employees to more than five hundred, and a family business model to a factory. But one thing that has not changed is Coach's belief that the key to having the right culture is hiring the right people.

Coach has a term he uses to describe the people he respects the most: butt-busters. I've heard him say a thousand times, "That guy, he's a butt-buster."

Here are the traits of a butt-buster:

1. *Character.* Key questions we ask about potential employees are, What type of person are they? Is there a pattern of loyalty? Are

they a team-first or me-first person? Will they be a fountain for our team or a drain?

2. *Heart.* We evaluate how much potential employees care about what they will do at our company. We want their job to be more than a job. Someone with heart will be willing to come in early, stay late, and go the extra mile to do whatever it takes to get the job done. We aren't interested in hiring someone who will simply be a clock puncher.

3. *Talent.* Talent ranks third because talent is often teachable, whereas the first two traits are not as easily taught. Of course, talent is important. Most of the folks working for our team are the best of the best in their areas, whether they are welders, fabricators, engineers, or race car drivers. But talent alone does not fit the Joe mold.

In our early years, we hired a young engineer who was one of the most talented engineers our company has ever had. On the smart scale, he was off the charts. He also was a very hard worker. Two boxes checked. But because he was negative and gossiped, he was like a cancer inside the team, the ultimate drain. That ended up outweighing the positives, and we let him go.

Was it difficult to dismiss someone with his talent? Yes and no. Yes, because we had invested in him, and he offered a lot as an engineer. We hoped he would change from a drain to a fountain, but he didn't. Drains rarely do. On the other hand, that decision was not difficult because of our commitment to being a company of employees who fit the Joe mold. Coach's hiring formula positions everyone on the team to succeed. What a drain subtracts from the team far outweighs what his talent adds, because he pulls the rest of the team members down from performing at their best.

Talent is a tease. In a sport built on being the fastest, where you're competing against the most talented teams in the world who are all trying to go faster than you, the temptation is to hire people who will help you go fast without considering their intangible qualities. That's a difficult trap to avoid because of the tendency to think, *We can rehabilitate this person.* The reality is, more often than not, you cannot. That's not exclusive to our sport. In other sports, a general manager, president, coach, or whoever the decision maker is also faces the temptation of thinking they can take a high-talent player with character issues and mold the character. I'm as much a sports fan as I am a professional working in sports, and from both observation and experience, I know that approach rarely works. Sports history books are littered with stories of teams that were uber-talented but train wrecks in character and heart. Many executives and coaches have lost their jobs because they fell for the tease of talent.

That's not to say we don't give people second chances. One of the rewarding aspects of my position is that I can sometimes help a person turn their life around. Generally, second chances come after someone makes a mistake. Mistakes are easier to forgive and move on from than character flaws. A person who is dishonest or a gossip or a drain is difficult to change.

By and large, people's tendencies are their tendencies for a reason. Some people inherently are not hard workers. Some aren't as passionate about their jobs as we would like to see. Those traits are more difficult to learn than skills. We attend school to learn skills, but there aren't many schools offering degrees in character, heart, and work ethic.

As a Redskins fan, I watched Coach take a team relying on free agents let go by other teams and lead it to the Super Bowl. I remember hearing his stories about recruiting free agents to the Redskins and evaluating potential draft picks. He didn't check only with players' college coaches; he talked to their high school coaches, youth-league coaches, and other people who knew them well, so that Coach could identify patterns that would indicate they would be a great player in his locker room. On the other hand, if a player caused trouble in college, Coach checked with his coaches at lower levels to see if that behavior was a pattern or an exception. In most cases, tendencies that pointed toward trouble revealed themselves before the college level.

Ultimately, Coach looked for patterns that foretold a player who would come to practice early, stay late, give everything he could for the organization, and be a great team player. Coach wanted to find a college coach who would tell him, "You're going to have a coach on the field with this guy." He wanted to find the high school coach who would tell him, "I've had faster guys and I've had guys who can jump higher, but he's the best locker room guy I've ever had."

"Find that pattern," Coach would say, "and those are the people you want to surround yourself with."

Coach's knack for identifying those types of players came from working hard to find them.

When Coach watched game film during the preseason, a game could be in the final minutes and the outcome well in hand, but he would keep rewinding and watching special teams plays. He watched not only his players to determine who he would keep and cut from the roster but also players from the opposing team who could be potential free agents.

"On special teams late in preseason games are where you find the kids that will kill for your team," he'd say. "Who are the guys who are going 100 percent, who are knocking people's heads and don't care that we already knew who was going to win and lose? That's the guy I want in the bunker with me."

I've also heard him say, "They're all great athletes at this level. So if I have five guys who are close in talent, I want the guy who's giving maximum effort when we're losing by twenty points with a minute left."

At JGR, we've had meetings about hiring a crew chief, and Coach would tell us, "Go find three people in our building who have worked for him and find out what kind of leader he is and what he's like to work for." With every job candidate, Coach wants to know, "Is this person going to enhance our culture or hurt our culture?" And "Can we learn from this person, or are they going to always take from us?" He wants to find the pattern that reveals whether a potential hire is a butt-buster.

Sometimes, I think "butt-buster" for Coach equates to "who works the most hours," because Coach is old school and values those who aren't afraid to put in the time. It's easy in football and racing, and in many other industries too. I have had to wrestle with Coach on that part many times, because in football, he and his coaches would grind in the same room hour after hour. When they left, they weren't answering texts and emails and running a company. In our business, as in most businesses, there are ways to be smart about getting your work done. I have tried to "manage up" to Coach and teach him that while hard work is key, it's possible to work smarter. Long hours are often included, but they are not the gold standard.

Based on Coach's example, the most important thing for me as a leader when it comes to hiring is to surround myself with people in leadership positions who have a pattern of working in the Joe mold. I've managed to make a career out of trying to never be the smartest person in the room. This isn't saying much given my intelligence level. Seriously: I don't say this to be self-effacing, but I do not consider myself to be the best at anything here. I'm not the best at math. I'm not the smartest businessperson. But I surround myself with people who are better than me in different areas.

> Great leaders are not afraid to surround themselves with people who are smarter in different areas.

I appreciate how Coach doesn't equate character with matching a certain personality profile. Talk to him about his favorite players from his Redskins days, and Gary Clark's and John Riggins's names likely will come up. Those guys had big personalities and could be a little out there sometimes. But Coach didn't mind. He wasn't looking for robots. He likes butt-busters with their own unique personalities.

Coach hires for character, because strong-character people with big personalities will make sure their personalities fit within a team-first culture.

We have hired two talented drivers who came to us with strong, distinct personalities. Tony Stewart came to us in 1999 when we added a second car. Kyle Busch started racing for us in 2008.

Tony won two Cup Series championships during his ten seasons with us. In 2020, he was honored with enshrinement into the NASCAR Hall of Fame alongside Coach and another one of our former drivers, Bobby Labonte. Kyle also has won two Cup championships. With a lot of career potentially still ahead for Kyle, he already is in the conversations debating the best drivers in NASCAR history.

Tony was known for possessing a temper that sometimes led to confrontations with other drivers and media members. He once described himself as "a fifteen-year-old trapped in a thirty-four-year-old body." Kyle is aggressive, opinionated, with the same fire as Tony, which at times can be quite difficult to deal with. His nickname, Rowdy, came from the antagonist character in the movie *Days of Thunder*.

When Tony and Kyle came to JGR, Coach let them be themselves. Some days, that decision worked to Coach's detriment. Those two guys collectively have probably caused Coach more hours of angst than any two other humans in history. But he resisted trying to turn them into corporate clones, because he loved their passion, their hearts, and their remarkable talents. In Tony and Kyle, Coach saw two generational talents with patterns of being singularly focused on being the best. They didn't come to us with patterns of just wanting to win races; they had demonstrated that they wanted to lead every lap.

Coach was not going to suppress their God-given personalities. Instead, he wanted to tap into their passion in a way that lifted the competitiveness of their crew members. Inserting one person who is, above all, committed to the mission tells the team members around them that you are committed to the mission too. In our case, when we put Tony and Kyle into cars, the crew members on those cars knew that every weekend, they would be working with a driver who not only wanted to win as much as anyone else at the track but who also had the talent most of the other teams didn't.

Part of being a butt-buster is being tough. Kyle earned the racing world's respect in 2015 after suffering a traumatic crash in the season opener that left him hospitalized with a broken right leg and broken left foot. He vowed to be back racing that season. Not only did Kyle come back twelve weeks later, but he also won his first Cup Series championship that year.

Coach loves those guys. I admire both for their uncanny focus and desire to win. I would need an entire chapter to list the things Tony did to help others during his time with us, most of it behind the scenes with no public recognition. He has a kind, generous heart.

Working with Tony and Kyle has taught me to be cautious about sticking labels on anyone. Both arrived with reputations of being difficult. But I've observed that having high standards and an incessant drive to win are markedly different. Although that has come with a degree of difficulty, it's been worth dealing with because of their roles in our mission.

We can be quick to slap the label of *diva* on an athlete, artist, or celebrity when the reality is that they want to be surrounded with the level of excellence at which they perform, and they don't respond well when they aren't.

## Hiring Up

Hiring internal and external candidates comes with different considerations for maintaining a company's culture. When my twin sons entered business school, I attended their orientation and was stunned to hear that the typical résumé gets looked at for eight seconds. An entire career, education, activities, and experiences can come down to the impression created with a potential employer in an eight-second scan of a piece of paper. Thus, the importance of networking, whether hiring or trying to be hired. Filling a role is much easier when a potential employee can be vouched for beyond the résumé—especially if the goal is not to just fill a spot but to improve it.

In my early days as a hiring manager, when expanding meant creating positions, I wanted to handpick from cultures and places that would add to our company. I enjoyed hiring people from corporate NASCAR because they brought a breadth of knowledge about how our sport worked and relationships within the industry that proved strategic for us.

The person I hired to replace me in licensing, J.J. Damato, had ten years of experience with NASCAR and ten years with the NHL. In other words, the unpaid intern who learned licensing on his own was upgraded by someone with two decades of experience in two major sports. I hired up.

For the first decade and a half of our company, we operated without a true public relations department. I oversaw PR until we made the decision in 2008 to create that department, meaning we didn't have the luxury of promoting from within. We hired Chris Helein to fill that role for two reasons. First, he was handling PR for the Washington Redskins when we hired him, so he understood the pressures of a professional sport. Second, he had earned Coach's trust while working with him in the trenches with the Redskins.

All communications, and especially public relations, are vital functions of a company. A CEO and the PR person must build a relationship that leads to trust, because when crisis hits, credibility is crucial. The PR director has to think and sometimes speak in the same vein as the CEO. He or she also needs to be able to ask the CEO the difficult questions that often are being asked within the company or about the company externally. Building that type of relationship takes time, and by going outside to hire Chris, we brought in someone who had already put in that time with Coach.

In both cases, filling my roles presented an opportunity to move the company forward. We didn't just hire someone to *fill* a role; we hired someone to *expand* a role. We hired up.

> Hire people not just to fill roles but to expand them.

The best way to maintain culture, though, is to grow your own talent. When a role is filled from outside an organization, particularly in senior management, that new leader will bring the corporate culture from the place they left. That provides a boost when they're bringing in the best of their previous company's culture. But ensuring that leadership carries the same vision as the owner or CEO is often best accomplished through promoting people from within.

Part of maintaining a company's culture also includes managers who understand that not every employee wants to move up into management positions. Managers reach their level because of their career ambitions, but good managers realize that their employees' ambitions can look different from theirs. Some employees want to stay in the jobs they're good at.

We can have fabricators who don't want to manage the fab shop and welders who don't want to manage the welding department. They want to fabricate and weld and do that well for a long time. The simple math is that not everyone can become a manager. I've had to learn this lesson over the years, and I've come to value the employees who are satisfied with the level they have reached. Their reasons can vary. Sometimes an employee is dealing with personal circumstances that make them content with their current role, responsibilities, and hours. Some people don't want the stress of a promotion or the additional responsibility. Others simply love doing what they already are doing.

But for the rest, there is no doubt that promoting from within has resulted in longevity with our employees, because there is a path for employees to move up. As I write, all four of our Cup crew chiefs worked their way up as engineers or as crew chiefs on our Xfinity Series teams. We've found that our employees tend to stay here if they know there is an opportunity to advance rather than leave for an offered opportunity with another team.

A great example of hiring from within is Byron Goggin, a drummer in a band who was hired early on to drive show cars for us. Byron has a great personality and loved to travel and talk to folks. After many years on the road, Byron worked his way into the front office, working with sponsors. He now oversees all the account managers at the track and handles several of our biggest accounts. He also has what we joke is the hardest job at Joe Gibbs Racing—he is in charge of Coach on race day, which means getting Coach where he needs to go from the minute he arrives until he leaves for the plane. That's a stressful job, I promise you. Byron has always delivered value to us because he is not afraid to do the little things and is someone who has never said, "That's not my job."

Sometimes the most fun position to fill is a created one. We can't hire up because we are starting from scratch, but we still are upgrading our company and our expertise in an area anytime we can add a new spot and hire a person we anticipate will grow within our company. A bonus is creating not only a new position but a new department. In 2009, we did that when we jumped into the world of social media.

At the time, no NASCAR team employed a social media person. I don't even recall *social media* being a common term then or many pro sports teams utilizing Facebook or Twitter. Most of our content for connecting with our fan base was on the team website.

Our data showed that Sunday—race day and our most important day of the week—was our slowest day for website traffic, and that bothered me. NASCAR's website received heavy traffic on race days because it was the only place fans could find live race coverage online, mostly in the form of lap-by-lap timing and scoring. Our website was static. I compared our website and other teams' sites at that point to a highway visitors center: a nice place to get some information once, but not a place to go back to—and certainly not for breaking news. I wanted our website to become a Sunday destination and envisioned the website taking on an entirely new look exclusively for race days. I wanted a person who on race days could serve a role similar to an AM radio, hometown broadcaster of a race by blogging behind-the-scenes information and play-by-plays for our drivers.

As we discussed what kind of person we needed to hire, we weren't even sure what we were looking for. No other NASCAR team employed anyone in that type of position, so we were starting without a template. Did we need a writer? A traditional public relations person? A website designer or a programmer? Someone who would become a company voice communicating directly with fans? We did know, though, that we would have to go outside the company to fulfill our online goals.

The social media world has grown so much since then that I have to laugh at how broad our search process was. I remember one of our leading candidates was an Applebee's manager who had writing experience. We had no idea what to look for.

We ended up hiring a fresh-out-of-college kid named Bryan Cook. Few people in racing circles know him by that name. Bryan had a big, curly hairstyle and a goatee that made him look just like NASCAR driver Boris Said. Joey Logano was a rookie driver for us in the Nationwide Series at the time, and during Bryan's first week on the job, Joey pointed out the resemblance and informed him that Boris was his new nickname. The name stuck.

We ended up hiring Boris based on a gut feeling. He had grown up a race fan and had a passion for racing. That is not always a plus when hiring, but it was for this job. He had studied art in college and possessed a rare combination of strong skills in writing, graphic design, and website design.

"I want you to be biased, and I want you to be opinionated," I told Boris. "I want you to be the eyes and ears for our employees, sponsors, and fans who aren't at the race. Tell them the story. Let them see behind the curtain—take them on the team plane, in the pits, even riding in the car with Coach into the track. Make the fans feel like they are part of the team, and when the race starts, tell them more than they would know if they were at the race in person."

I also strongly believe that companies don't talk; people do. I wanted people to get to know Boris as their contact inside the company.

Within two weeks, Sunday had become our website's highest-traffic day of the week, and Boris had become a near-celebrity. When the social media boom hit, our company rode atop the first wave because we had a person on the ground embedded in our culture. A few years ago, when a social media company approached NASCAR about attending a race on a learning expedition, the company asked to meet with three people: Dale Earnhardt Jr., Jimmie Johnson, and Boris. All three are NASCAR stars in my book.

Boris didn't fit the typical mold of a race team, but he and JGR turned out to be a perfect match. He now is our chief digital officer and has a team of folks in his department, and he represents our company by speaking at seminars about how to employ social platforms to tell stories. As Boris describes it, engaging on social media is simply meeting with fans in the places they choose to congregate.

Boris, like so many others in our front office, came in and made us better. The principle is clear: whether bringing in someone from the outside or promoting from within, always hire up.

## TOPICS FOR REFLECTION

1. Part of creating a winning culture is hiring the right people. Coach hires people who fit "the Joe mold," "butt-busters" with character, heart, and talent. How does your organization prioritize character, heart, and talent in the hiring process?
2. Would you describe yourself as a butt-buster? If so, in what ways? If not, identify three ways in which you could immediately start becoming a butt-buster.
3. Among your coworkers, who would you say is a butt-buster? What qualities make them a butt-buster?

## Chapter 8

# BUYING IN TO A CULTURE OF YES

WE AREN'T BUILDING BRIDGES OR CURING CANCER—we are racing cars to provide entertainment. That's something I remind myself of when I feel like we are taking ourselves too seriously.

I have spent my career in customer service. We race cars, but for many of us in the front office who don't touch the cars, our jobs are to bring in revenue and keep our partners happy. We must provide value for our partners as a marketing platform, or we no longer exist. Therefore, I am ultimately in the customer service business, and you know the saying: the customer is *always* right.

A culture of yes means entering every interaction with a posture of wanting to serve the customer. That does not mean saying yes regardless of what they ask for. It does mean underpromising and overdelivering. (Sounds like delivering more value to customers than they pay for, right?) It means *never* pulling out a contract when there is an issue with a customer—and I haven't in my nearly thirty-year career. It means approaching everything with an expectation to please the customer, and when you can't, trying to make something work instead of leading with no.

My introduction to the phrase "a culture of yes" came from our friends at Toyota. A few years into our partnership, Ed Laukes, one of Toyota's head executives who oversees marketing and advertising, asked Todd and me to come see him at their headquarters in Torrance, California. (Toyota has since relocated to Plano, Texas.) Toyota, like most customers, appreciates meeting face-to-face, and Todd and I made a point of visiting as often as possible.

When Todd and I arrived at Toyota's offices, we exchanged pleasantries, but I could tell something was bothering Ed. Not long into our meeting, he directly told us, "You know what your problem is? You guys at Joe Gibbs Racing have a culture of no."

Yikes! Not what I wanted to hear from our biggest partner. We could have countered, "We have the best sponsors in the business; they are all happy, and we win races for you. So what's the problem?" Instead, we listened and took notes as Ed walked us through a list of examples that were all legitimate.

A key to good customer service is making each customer feel like they are the most important one. In the case of our meeting at Toyota, we learned that we weren't doing a good enough job of letting them know we realize they are our biggest partner. We were doing a *good* job with our relationship but not a *great* job. We were winning on the track, yet we had lost sight of the fact that our relationship with Toyota was as important as our cars' performance. We needed to be creating more value for Toyota than it paid for, and we were missing the mark.

After our meeting, we went to dinner and laughed and had a great meal together, demonstrating that much like personal relationships, the business of relationships is about being able to have honest, difficult discussions geared toward making the relationship stronger.

But that one statement—"You have a culture of no"—changed our front office philosophy. Todd and I spent the entire trip home strategizing how we could fix our problems. We needed to strengthen the relationship with our biggest partner at every level. Not just one thing would improve the relationship; we needed to focus on dozens of smaller things, including better communication, saying thank you more often, and being more intentional about meeting Toyota's objectives.

Based on Toyota's feelings, we determined that we likely needed to make ourselves better all around. We talked with each of our partners about how we could change their perception of us. We needed to create a culture of yes, and we did.

A culture of yes looks like this: treating every partner, from smallest to largest, like they are our only customer. It means exceeding their expectations in even the smallest things. It means being proactive by doing things even when they don't ask. Then when they do make a request, it means receiving the request with the absolute intention of either making it happen or delivering a better alternative. But most important, a culture of yes means constantly communicating to the customer, at every level within the organization, that they matter, that they are important, and that we go to bed and wake up thinking about how we can deliver value to them.

I am grateful that Ed was willing to initiate a tough conversation that resulted in us raising our game not only for Toyota but for all our partners.

## Knowing and Communicating the "Why"

To win in business and in life we need to ask the question, "What's my why?" Winning businesses are the ones that communicate clear answers to that question.

For Joe Gibbs Racing, the "why" that drives everything for us is the "honoring God" part of our culture. We believe we are to do everything with excellence, so why would we not relentlessly pursue being great?

Also, we know that in the grand scheme of things, trophies and records are nice, but they aren't enough in and of themselves. What's important is that they provide a platform to do bigger and better things.

The more races we win, the more charities we can support. JGR supports nearly one hundred ministry organizations around the world. The more we win, the more we earn a platform to influence people: our fans, our racing community, our world. Performance equals influence, and making a positive influence particularly in the ministry area is the why that motivates our company every day.

This makes sense for an organization, but we also should understand our why on an individual level. Part of delivering more than you cost is understanding why you do what you do. For me, I want to use whatever talents God has given me in an environment that grows me, where I can invest in people, increase my personal influence, and provide a good life for my family. That's my why for going to work every day.

With each phase of my career, the why has become increasingly important. Securing the next deal or winning the next race doesn't fill my tank the way it used to. I seek purpose, and I want what I do to matter on a broader scale. Each person has their own why, and each person's why can be very different. Understanding, respecting, and appreciating one another—even those who don't think or believe like us—make up an important component of every corporate culture.

For business leaders, remembering the big-picture why needs to be accompanied by communicating the smaller why—the reasons we do things in our day-to-day decisions.

> The pursuit of success is important not just for our own gratification, but because success leads to a bigger platform, and a bigger platform leads to more influence in areas we value.

Part of our internal communications strategy at JGR is to over-communicate and always answer the why on our major decisions. Explaining to our employees and partners why we make certain decisions or take certain actions is important on numerous levels.

I see too many businesses that underestimate how much people simply want to be communicated with—specifically, addressing the why for corporate decisions and actions. People want to belong to a company, an organization, or a cause that is about more than themselves, and they want to feel like they matter. When a company is secretive and hides information, employees will begin to believe they don't matter. The best way to make someone feel they are important is to communicate openly and honestly with them as much as possible. Whether the communication occurs company-wide, to a department, or with an individual, open and honest communication sends the message "You matter enough for me to take the time to talk to you."

A good example is our approach each time we added a team. Current employees and sponsor partners were not generally excited each time we expanded. After all, more people and more partners would in theory mean less time and attention for the existing ones. Thus, communicating the why behind our expansion was crucial.

We intentionally overcommunicated to our employees not only about what we were doing to grow but also about why we were growing. We were up front in stating that the biggest factor in our decision to add teams was survival. The NASCAR model is that teams must raise 75 to 80 percent of their revenue through sponsorships. The landscape was changing. Racing at the level we needed to was becoming more expensive, and it was difficult to increase revenue at the proportionate rate.

To continue winning races, we needed to raise more money. Raising more money required winning. We determined that to continue winning would require adding scale to our operations.

Our options boiled down to grow or go out of business. We had to communicate to our employees and sponsors that growth would mean better performance for them. It's the old concept of a rising tide lifting all boats. Growth also meant new business partners to work with, which would create more opportunities for our sponsors to work together with the new companies coming in.

Getting buy-in on the why was essential to maintaining our culture during each growth period. We held Q and A sessions with our employees and encouraged them to raise their concerns and ask any questions they wanted. Then when the first few questions were asked, we answered openly and honestly to demonstrate that we truly were granting permission to voice concerns and ask questions.

The truth of business is that when we executives announce grandiose plans that get us all excited about the possibilities, the biggest concern for most employees is how our plans will affect them as individuals. When we expanded, employees wanted to know whether they would be able to find a parking spot each morning, if their pay would be impacted, and how building more parts would affect overall quality. Those were quality-of-life questions for our employees, and they deserved our attention.

From my perspective, creating avenues for two-way communication demonstrated that we were confident in our decision and cared enough about our employees that we considered them partners with shared interest in the company's success. In addition to our company-wide meetings, we assigned managers the responsibility of further communicating our why with their employees on a more direct level.

Sometimes it is more difficult to communicate the why. We often hold confidential meetings about changing a driver or bringing on a new sponsor, and we cannot tell our employees until the last minute. In some cases, we need to explain the why after a decision or change has been made. The frustration that results is understandable. Regardless of the timing, explaining the why to the extent we are able is always a good idea.

When a company is silent, people will invent their own why. A void of information is filled by assumption, and that's dangerous. Employees will arrive at their own conclusions because people always talk to each other, and a narrative *will* develop within the company.

In our case, a lack of information could have resulted in conversations like this:

"I heard through the grapevine that we're hiring a bunch of people."
"Does that mean we're firing a bunch of people?"
"I don't know. They haven't talked to me."
"Why are we doing this?"
"Must be to make more money, because they're not talking to us about it."

Management can either guide the narrative or inherit the narrative. People want to be communicated with honestly. For us the open and honest way in which Coach communicates and the confidence he expresses when he talks have allowed us to maintain a culture in which our employees and partners typically buy in to the why.

## Protect Your Brand

Nothing is more important than a good name. The quality of a person's reputation dictates their level of influence. What do you value? Are you consistent in every aspect of your life? Is your word your bond or just words? How do you treat people? Wrapped up in our reputation is the accumulation of hundreds of small actions over the course of our lives.

Similarly, nothing is more important to a company than its good name.

Brand names take years to build but can be destroyed by a single person or event. When that brand name is the name of a family founder, like Disney or Hilton or Joe Gibbs Racing, protecting a brand's reputation is even more critical.

> Brands take years to build but can be destroyed by a single person or event, so guard them carefully.

Coach's personal version of new employee orientation is pretty simple, and he repeats it to every new employee: "There's only one name on the shirt that you wear, and it's mine. It's Joe Gibbs Racing. So use common sense, and don't embarrass me."

That advice is simple, fairly broad, and, I admit, intimidating.

Coach has worked his entire life building up his reputation. That reputation grew like a bank account by making thousands of small deposits. Over a long period of time, he has strived to be consistent, practice what he preaches, and live and work with integrity. One mistake by someone wearing a shirt with his name on it can cause a massive withdrawal from that account.

The nature of NASCAR can make that a slippery slope for us. There's an old NASCAR expression that says, "If you ain't cheatin', you ain't tryin'." I don't like that sentiment. NASCAR rules intentionally create a gray area in which teams compete with each other. The rules contain black-and-white lines that, when crossed, leave no doubt that a team is breaking the rules to gain an unfair advantage. But as anyone who has worked around cars knows, the nature of the beast is that not every parameter can be precisely defined. Wiggle room is necessary, and it's within that wiggle room that teams focus time and resources to find extra speed.

The NASCAR rule book, even as thick as it is, cannot account for everything. That's where the brilliance of the engineers and mechanics comes into play. The difference between those who figure out how to go the fastest is not only the difference between first place and second place. In this era of multicar teams and teams aligning to share information and technology, the difference could be between first place and twentieth place. Or more.

Being creative in the gray areas is an art form in NASCAR.

Coach is adamant that while we push as hard as we can, everyone in the building must know not to cross the line. He preaches all the time that we need to win the right way—within the rules.

In 2008, we learned how quickly one poor decision could damage our entire company's reputation. Before Toyota began manufacturing engines for our teams, we built our own. Two of our cars failed post-race inspections in what then was called the Nationwide Series (now Xfinity Series) because of two well-intentioned employees who suffered a bad lapse in judgment.

At that time, Cup Series drivers regularly raced in Nationwide Series races. Nationwide sponsors liked having the big-name drivers tied to their cars, and most Cup drivers believed they benefited from racing in the shorter race the day before the Cup race. Between Tony Stewart, Kyle Busch, Denny Hamlin, and Joey Logano, our two-car Nationwide team had won fifteen of the first twenty-four races entering the weekend at Michigan International Speedway.

NASCAR makes in-season adjustments in order to do what it feels is best to create a level playing field. A few weeks earlier, NASCAR had issued a change requiring Toyota's Nationwide teams to use a smaller spacer that would cut back horsepower in their motors by 15 percent. (I'm a marketing guy, and that is as technical as I get.)

The new requirement didn't sit well in our shop. Our guys felt like we were behind other teams in one of the gray areas concerning engines, but they had found a way to create an advantage in another one of those gray areas to make up for it. We thought NASCAR was trying to create parity in one area while overlooking another area with clear disparity. Imagine the International Olympic Committee telling Usain Bolt that he was too fast compared to the others so he would have to wear ankle weights to give other sprinters a better chance to win. That's how we felt.

Our advantage came as the result of smart, hardworking employees, and even though NASCAR said the new rule was not a matter of picking on us or Toyota for being good at our jobs, the sentiment in the shop said otherwise.

NASCAR inspects cars after each race, and as its inspectors prepared to test the horsepower on our two Nationwide cars, they found magnets under the accelerators. Two of our employees had decided to mask how good our engines were by placing a quarter-inch magnet under each gas pedal. When the cars were hooked up to the engine-testing machine, the magnets would prevent the engines from reaching maximum acceleration.

The employees' actions did nothing to improve our performance during the race. (Our cars placed third and seventh.) Instead, they cheated on the post-race test. Nonetheless, they cheated.

Immediately following the discovery of the magnets, a stunned Coach and J.D. took full responsibility through media interviews and apologized for the two employees' actions. Coach said the way our employees should have responded to the horsepower restrictions was to win the season championship by working within the new rules. Unfortunately, that's not the route the two employees chose.

A few days after the race, NASCAR handed down significant penalties against our team that included suspensions for both crew chiefs and five other crew members and probations for both drivers. Seven individuals were named in the penalties for the offenses committed by two people acting on their own. We also were fined points in the driver and owner standings that determine season championships. After NASCAR announced the penalties, our team added a monetary fine to emphasize our hard stance against cheating.

When we investigated the cheating internally, the two said their intent was to protect the company. Clearly, their actions produced the opposite effect. We announced our own suspension of the two employees plus took other disciplinary actions that we did not make public. We held serious discussions about their futures with our company. Strong arguments were made to fire them, especially the one who admitted to leading the effort. I must say that, typically, their actions would have been a fireable offense. But in that instance, Coach opted to show them grace because they—again, foolishly—thought they were helping JGR and their actions were out of line with the patterns they had established as our employees. They had a history of being team guys and were part of the family. Coach added as he told us his decision, however, that if their actions had made even the slightest impact on the race, no discussion would have been necessary. They would have been terminated.

Still, they damaged our team's name and reputation. I remember reading on the SportsCenter ticker, "Joe Gibbs Racing caught cheating." All the headlines were about Joe Gibbs Racing, not the two employees. Our success to that point in the season was called into question. Those who didn't understand that the cheating had occurred on the testing rather than the cars' performance wrongly assumed that we had been winning because we were cheating. All our hard work was being dismissed by the public, replaced with "They must have been cheating all along" commentaries.

The actions of two people impacted hundreds of others. The effect was felt even outside of our offices. My wife was at the grocery store, and someone Stacey had not seen in years came up to her and asked, "How does it feel to have your husband work for a cheater?"

*What?*

JGR was established on Christian principles. Coach has spent his whole life building a reputation of integrity. It was amazing to see how a company's reputation could transform from exemplary to shady with just one action. And regardless of motive.

That's why you don't cheat. You don't cheat on an engine test. You don't cheat your company by taking care of personal business while on the clock. You don't cheat on even one item on an expense report. A reputation should be protected like a prized possession.

Because of that one poor decision, the "cheaters" tag shadowed us for a few years.

**Reputation Triage**

That cheaters accusation resurfaced when we experienced another controversy in 2013.

Matt Kenseth won the STP 400 at Kansas Speedway for our fourth victory in the first eight races of the Cup season. When the car underwent testing at NASCAR's Research and Development Center, one of the eight connecting rods that connected the pistons to the crankshaft was discovered to be 3 grams under the minimum required weight of 525 grams. For comparison's sake, a penny weighs about 3 grams. The penalties against Kenseth, crew chief Jason Ratcliff, and Coach were among the most severe NASCAR had ever handed down.

The weight of that one rod did not give us a competitive advantage during the race. At least two drivers from competing teams spoke publicly in our defense. If someone had wanted to go outside the specifications on the connecting rods, they would have gone heavier, not lighter, to make the rods more durable, because a broken rod leads to replacing the engine in a car.

Toyota Racing Development was providing the engines for our three Cup cars, as they do today, and TRD had not built the batch of connecting rods for those cars. They had purchased them from an outside vendor and placed them inside the engine. TRD immediately stepped up to accept the blame for the too-light rod, saying that the part had arrived from the vendor at the wrong weight and the mistake had gone unnoticed by TRD.

But still, those words came back: "Joe Gibbs Racing is a bunch of cheaters!"

A couple of our sponsors were forced to field calls from people complaining they were sponsoring cheaters.

We exercised our right to appeal to an independent panel of three people who currently or had previously worked in the industry. During the hearing, we accepted that the rod was illegal but claimed the penalties were too severe considering that the terms of our lease agreement on engines prohibited us from touching anything inside the engine.

At that time, roughly two-thirds of NASCAR appeals were upheld. But the panel agreed with our contention and drastically reduced the penalties.

I was probably as mad about that incident as I've ever been in my career. To this day, Coach occasionally brings up that story and how angry we were. It was like being handed a life sentence for driving twenty-six in a twenty-five. One piece of the punishment was subtracting fifty points from our team in the owner standings. That punishment alone could have cost us the end-of-season championship and, as a result, more than a million dollars. Sponsors understandably asked us difficult questions. Losing one major sponsor could have meant laying off dozens of employees. That means dozens of families would have had their lives turned upside down. We had to fight not only for our company's reputation but also for our employees' livelihoods.

NASCAR, to its credit, revamped its penalty process because the damage we suffered showed how much is at stake in a sponsorship-driven sport. But going through that experience revealed how big of an undeserved withdrawal one incident can take from a company's reputation. More people will hear about the initial bad news than will hear about the reversed, positive outcome. There is rarely a scrolling ticker with the confession "We were wrong—they didn't cheat."

Those two problems came from different sources: one was poor judgment, the other an honest mistake we had no control over. Regardless, the damage to a good reputation—fair or not—took a long time to repair.

## The Impact of Buy-In

JGR began in a tiny ten-thousand-square-foot rented building running one car. I believe that's what Coach thought he was committing to when he created the team—a small group of employees doing a little bit of everything in a garage and going out to lunch together for fun.

Now, we have more than five hundred employees working in a 400,000-square-foot building that we own. We have sixty-five *managers*—more than three times the number of employees we had when we started. We field four cars in the Cup Series and three in the Xfinity Series. We run two development cars in ARCA and two motocross teams.

At the start, we didn't have a devoted engineer; now we employ more than sixty engineers. Back then, our team drove to races six hours or less from home and flew commercial to the others. Now, we have an aviation department and fly 150 people to races every week on three jets. We employ our own pilots, flight attendants, and mechanics. Back then, we bought car parts from vendors. Now, we make 95 percent of our parts in-house.

We have evolved into a collection of companies, including a manufacturing facility, an engineering company, an aviation business, a boutique marketing firm, and a social media agency. All under the umbrella of a NASCAR team.

Each time we have expanded, the growth has been calculated and evaluated. It started with Coach's mastery of knowing how to build teams and motivate people. He recognized as we added cars and employees that if we were to be a team, we would have to be the same team. He knew that every employee would need to have skin in the game. They would need to buy in to our culture and what we do.

Ninety percent of the people in our building do not work on one specific car. We face no challenge in getting them to feel like part of the victory when any of our drivers wins. But for the other 10 percent, like the guys who travel with each car, even those folks have an incentive with the other cars. Are they mad when the other drivers win? Of course. They all want to win. And with ten laps to go in a race, we want each of our teams wanting to win.

The two unwritten rules in NASCAR at the end of a race are don't wreck a teammate and don't help someone else beat your teammate. But other than that, we want our drivers doing what it takes for them to win the race. Believe me, any driver finds a little extra gratification in beating his teammates at the end of the race because they're essentially racing in the same equipment, and the winner is the one who drove his equipment better.

But within that context, there are moments like the end of the 2019 Daytona 500 that illustrate what our four cars, one team culture looks like when everyone, including the drivers, buys in to that culture.

A series of late wrecks forced the race into overtime—two laps to determine the winner when the scheduled end of the race comes under a yellow caution flag. Denny Hamlin and Kyle Busch started the overtime in first and second place, respectively. Erik Jones was in seventh, making our three cars the only Toyotas in the top sixteen. Kyle slipped to fourth place early in the final lap before making a final run at Denny and moving back into second. When it became evident entering Turn 4 that Kyle would not be able to catch Denny, Kyle blocked Joey Logano (who was no longer driving with JGR) to ensure that Denny would win.

Kyle could have dipped low in the turn and tried to make a crazy move to potentially force Denny to slip up. That type of move had a low chance of success and also could have caused Denny to go low to block Kyle, which would have opened up the outside line to pass both of them at the finish and neither of them would have won. Instead, Kyle played the role of good teammate to Denny. As an added bonus, his block allowed Erik to make a late charge into third place for the best showing in the Daytona 500 of his young career. Our 1-2-3 finish marked the first time in twenty-two years that one team had swept the top three spots at Daytona.

Kyle might be the most competitive human on the planet, partly because I think he hates losing even more than he obsesses over winning. And a Daytona 500 championship is the most conspicuous absence among his career accomplishments. Our team is fully aware that Kyle has a massive trophy case with an empty shelf reserved for the Daytona 500 trophy. As that race ended, before going to Victory Lane to celebrate with Denny, I went to see Kyle as he climbed out of his car. I was the first person to get to him. He had just taken his helmet off when I walked up. Knowing how he loathes finishing second, I expected to find him fuming. He was.

"I just want you to know," I told him, "we wouldn't have won that race if you hadn't done what you did."

In typical Kyle fashion, he told me, "Yeah, great. I don't get a [bleeping] trophy for that, do I?"

I gave Kyle a fist bump that he didn't want and headed to Victory Lane to celebrate with Denny's team.

Later, a cooled-down Kyle said, "Coming off Turn 4, I knew if I wasn't going to win it, I had to make sure Joe Gibbs Racing won it."

That's buy-in to a culture. That's a Joe Gibbs guy.

To be clear, there's a difference between that and Kyle saying, "Coming off Turn 4, I let off the gas because I wanted Denny to win." That's not what we hire drivers to do. That's not why sponsors pour big money into their cars. We want our drivers trying to win every race. But Kyle's response was exactly how we want our teammates to race—do everything possible to win for yourself, your sponsor, and your fans while being mindful of your teammates. Kyle did both, and his split-second decision came as the result of being bought in to our culture. Kyle gets it.

For a driver to play the role Kyle played in the season's biggest race, he would need to have experienced the give and take of our sport—to have seen firsthand how other drivers have helped make him better and truly believe that, when the roles are reversed, he will be the one benefiting from a teammate.

That 1-2-3 finish also represented what Coach calls his biggest win of all time, regardless of sport. That's a bold statement from a guy who has won three Super Bowls and more than three hundred races in NASCAR. That Daytona 500 was our first race since J.D. had passed away, and our company was hurting. Our friends at Toyota and Fox had arranged for a tribute to J.D. during the race, on lap 11, to represent J.D.'s jersey number in football. Fox's broadcast would go silent for that lap as our teams held up signs honoring J.D. FedEx had purchased a full-page ad in *USA Today* honoring J.D., and their number 11 car had a tribute on the trunk that read "#DoItForJD."

And then there was the driver of the 11 car, Denny. J.D. had hired Denny, and the two became good friends. James Dennis Alan Hamlin altered the name over the door of his car to read "J.D. Hamlin" using J.D.'s signature. Denny also committed $111 for every lap he would lead that season to go to J.D.'s Legacy Fund. (He led 922.) I'll forever be grateful to Denny and FedEx for the way they honored my friend. We started the season with heavy hearts and needed to know everything was going to be okay.

So for *that* car to win *that* race, with Kyle and Erik right behind, was nothing short of miraculous. That's why Coach chose Denny's car from that victory to sit in the NASCAR Hall of Fame as the one representing his induction.

I will always cherish that night. To cry with Stacey and my sons, along with J.D.'s boys and Melissa, was a truly surreal moment.

In a completely different way, Tony Stewart bought in to our culture when he was driving for us, and he demonstrated it on his final day.

We have a tradition that we do for—perhaps I should say we do *to*—some of our outgoing employees. I don't remember how it started, but we hold a ceremony for a departing member of our team during which we duct-tape him to the flagpole in front of our office and leave him there for about an hour so that fans dropping in to visit can take a picture or pose for a photo with him.

Tony Stewart left JGR following the 2008 season. In the week of activities leading up to Tony's induction into the NASCAR Hall of Fame in 2020 alongside Coach, he gave a touching account of his departure. Tony asked for a release from the last year of his contract because he was presented with the opportunity to assume half ownership of the Haas CNC Racing team now known as Stewart-Haas Racing. In media interviews leading up to the induction ceremonies, Tony shared part of his private conversation with Coach when he asked for his release. As Tony explained how he wanted to become part owner of a team, he told Coach, "This is my opportunity to be like you."

None of us wanted Tony to leave. He was a significant part of our team. But to hear the impact more than a decade later that Coach had on Tony and his desire to be like Coach as he moved into ownership affirmed the type of culture we strive to maintain.

Before Tony left, we managed to have a few laughs at his expense. Tony knew of our flagpole tradition, and he kept making funny threats about what he would do if we tried to prank him when he left.

But hey, tradition is tradition, right?

Four guys dressed up like sunglasses-wearing ninjas and trapped Tony in a room with no escape route. They tackled Tony and duct-taped him to a dolly and then rolled him outside and taped him to the flagpole. Tony play-fought the guys, but it was clear that he loved being treated just like anyone else at our company.

The funniest part was watching the reactions of fans as they realized Tony Stewart was duct-taped to the flagpole. Families started posing for pictures with Tony as he stood there unable to move his arms or legs. He enjoyed the interactions, laughing with every fan who talked with him. Tony was like any regular Joe Gibbs Racing employee.

Maintaining our culture requires relentless effort, and it is rewarding anytime we can see the fruit of that effort on display from one of our sport's highest-profile drivers.

Whether it's on NASCAR's biggest stage or taped to a flagpole.

## TOPICS FOR REFLECTION

1. Knowing and communicating the "why" of your organization is crucial for buy-in. More often than not, do you understand the why of your organization and do you feel bought in to it? Do you understand why you do what you do on a daily basis and where that fits in to the company's mission?

2. Reputation is built up gradually, like a bank account, through small deposits, but large withdrawals can quickly undo the work that has been done over time. What "deposits" can you make today in your personal reputation bank? In your organization's? What steps can you take to guard your reputation and that of your organization?

# STAY ON MISSION

## Chapter 9

# THE MOST IMPORTANT QUESTION

"Does this make us go fast?"

That one simple question has driven every decision we have made at Joe Gibbs Racing since day one, whether making a capital purchase, hiring an employee, or hosting a meeting.

Our relentless pursuit of going fast centers around the idea that as long as we go faster than everyone else, we will lead laps and win races, and then everything else will take care of itself. The day we stop going fast is the day everything crashes down.

Our two main sources of revenue are sponsorship (75 to 80 percent) and race purses (15 to 20 percent). When we sit down with a potential new partner, we sell them on a superior product through on-track performance and exceptional service off the track. We are not the low-cost provider. Our partners pay us a premium to win. They expect our cars to be on TV more than other teams' because we are leading more laps, winning more races, and staying in the upper echelon of our field, just as their brands are the leaders in their respective fields.

If we lose focus on going fast, our whole brand proposition will change, the caliber of brands wanting to work with us will change with it, and Joe Gibbs Racing will cease to be Joe Gibbs Racing. We *must* go fast.

That is why our third overarching principle is "Stay on mission."

> Every company needs a compass—
> a simple mission as its North Star guiding its journey.

When Coach entered NASCAR, he brought from his football experience the ability to pick key players for fulfilling the mission and then secured them with contracts. Contracts existed in NASCAR before we came along, but to help us stay on mission, Coach took the strategy around contracts in our sport to a new level. Anyone in a position that directly made our car go faster or was privy to our information on how we go fast was signed to a contract. The building was practically divided between contract employees and, well, people like me. I joke that we were the "expendable" ones. Or at least I was.

With most NASCAR teams located within twenty minutes of each other in the Charlotte area, it's not out of the ordinary for an employee to receive a job offer from a competing team, accept the offer, put his toolbox in his truck, and drive across town to start his new job—all without having to move or cause his kids to change schools. Imagine a pro sports league where teams were based in the same city, there were no free-agency restrictions, and year-round recruiting was an accepted practice. The pursuit of players would turn into a free-for-all. Welcome to NASCAR.

NASCAR is a wonderful, tight-knit community, but that lends itself to open recruiting. Employees of one team share neighborhoods with employees of other teams. Their kids go to school together and play on the same youth sports teams. Their families see each other on a regular basis at the grocery store, church, and restaurants. Spouses of team members do life together, and, of course, they talk.

Coach's move to increase the number of team members under contract led to us enjoying a turnover rate that probably was lower than all other teams for a period of time. Losing a critical employee presented a double negative because not only did we lose the bit of speed that person brought, but it also sent that speed to another team. Coach was resolute about keeping our people. If you helped us go fast, you weren't going anywhere.

We have always had to perform well to stay in business. Because Coach is not a businessman with outside resources as a safety net, we can only spend what we bring in through racing. Of the income we raise, we spend the largest percentage on what makes us go fast.

Staying on mission has required difficult conversations that have led to difficult decisions. Especially during our formative years.

Each fall, every department submitted reports with requests for capital purchases for the following year. Then we managers met and debated why each item was important and horse traded a little, if necessary. Our key question—"Does this make us go fast?"— guided our decisions. Each year, we rejected requests for items that we thought would be good for the company, because we had a finite amount of money to spend and going fast took priority. We all knew going into the meeting that our individual lists contained requests that wouldn't make the cut.

For fifteen years, we did not have a true public relations department. Marketing and PR was my area, but it did not directly make us go fast. I lobbied every year to expand that area, and year after year my request was denied. Marketing and PR was considered "nice to have," but until we had the scale to fund it, the choice was always to expand in areas that directly affected going fast.

The annual process helped create proper expectations so that we would likely leave a meeting disappointed we hadn't received an approval we wanted but convinced that everyone in the room was united in staying on mission.

## Sign of the Times

Longtimers here point to the sign in front of our current building as a symbol of our determination to stay on mission.

We moved into our present home in our sixth year. Outdoor signage requirements in our business park put a price tag of about $10,000 on us having a sign out front that said "Joe Gibbs Racing."

Each year as we worked through the list of requests during our budget meetings, the sign came up. Everyone in the room understood why we needed a sign. Fans came to visit and told us they had a difficult time finding us. Delivery drivers fussed about the lack of a sign. Partners visiting for the first time told us, "I couldn't find your building. Is there not a sign out front?"

Each year when we discussed a sign, we asked, "Does this make us go fast?" Each year, the answer was "No." Then once we had allocated the budget for our go-fast items, $10,000 to purchase a sign wasn't as important as everything else we considered.

That routine played out for more than five years—until a big sponsor told us, "You guys should really have a sign out front." We'd had a particularly good year financially, and the managers finally deemed a sign worthy of purchase.

Over that span, the sign and its annual rejection became a running joke within the office. "Maybe next year!" But the empty spot in front of our building where a sign should go also served as a symbol of our persistence in only purchasing what aligned with our mission. "If we aren't buying a sign, we definitely aren't buying *that*."

I have wanted to upgrade our lobby for the past ten years. Our lobby is nice. We have a "showroom floor" show car from each of our teams and a brand-new Toyota Camry on display, plus walls lined with trophy cases. But our lobby is not 2021 impressive. We are located twenty minutes from the NASCAR Hall of Fame, a showplace of our sport that is rendered with excellence. I wish we could provide a high-tech visitor experience on par with that.

The NASCAR Hall of Fame draws more than 150,000 visitors per year, and offering a complementary experience at our headquarters would be good for our fans, our company, and our partners from a marketing standpoint. But we operate lean every year on big-ticket items, and the high price tag to upgrade our lobby to that level does not fit within our mission.

Similarly, our auditorium seats about a hundred people. We hold meetings there, and fans can watch a video about JGR on their visits. The auditorium is nice, but it hasn't been upgraded in the twenty-plus years we have called this facility home. I desperately want to install new, fancy seats. Every year we anticipate our capital budget exceeding the list of items that make us go faster, but that doesn't seem to happen. As lean as we must operate, updating our auditorium might never be chosen over anything that makes us go fast.

Just as with the lack of a sign out front when we first moved into this building, resisting certain "would be nice to have" luxuries sets a tone in the building, because our employees know our commitment to the mission.

All that being said, a balance exists. Any area we believe is deficient or does not create a positive brand image of us and our partners gets shifted into the urgent, "mission critical" category.

And to be fair, we have an attractive lobby with a shiny floor and five sparkling cars on display. Our receptionist greets everyone with a smile and efficiency. Visitors are going to sit in a comfortable seat in our auditorium while watching our JGR highlight video. We care about the fan experience and how our building represents the excellence of our partners. But we draw the line where it affects the overall mission of going fast.

If we were a NASCAR museum, our budget would look completely different, and we would blow visitors away with our lobby and their overall experience. We're helped by remembering why fans come into our headquarters in the first place: they enjoy cheering for us because we win. The slickest lobby in the world wouldn't attract fans if we finished thirtieth every week. The best decoration we can give fans is a trophy and a victory banner, and we earn those by going faster than everyone else.

The possibility of a NASCAR salary cap like stick-and-ball sports have instituted to control spending is a real possibility. (So real that by the time this book is released, a spending cap could be in place.) As discussions of a potential salary cap have increased in intensity, I've stated all along that at JGR, we have always had a spending cap. Whatever revenue we bring in is our cap. If revenue goes down $1 million from one season to the next, we will have $1 million less to spend. During our financial discussions, we gather around the table and talk not only about what we won't buy but also about what we will cut without affecting our ability to go fast. Those are painstaking decisions because 70 percent of our expenses involve people. As best we can, we will make cuts in that other 30 percent that does not involve people. And because we must go fast, the cuts will be in areas that don't affect us on the track.

Our commitment to the mission also means going over budget when necessary. We are not a typical company in that manner. We meet about the budget every month to monitor where we are projecting over and under budget. During one of those meetings, the competition director might say, "We have a bad batch of spindles, and we'll have to make double the amount next quarter. And, by the way, this other race team just bought this piece of equipment, and if we don't buy one, they're going to kick our rear ends."

A typical company probably would say, "We'll just have to wait until next year to buy it." For us, the decision is clear: we are going to go over budget to make double the spindles and buy that piece of equipment. When those conversations come up during our meetings, going fast wins. (And those are the meetings when I'm glad I am not the CFO!) We must operate that way, even though doing so creates difficult situations for a family-owned business that doesn't have a backstop in place. The options are to go get more dollars in sponsorship or cut expenses in areas that don't make us go fast. We have survived that way for twenty-seven years.

Even as the scope of our business has radically changed with growth, the mission of going fast has remained unchanged.

**Controlling Our Destiny**

Imagine a football team leading by thirty points late in the fourth quarter and losing on a fluke play in the last second. Sounds ridiculous because it can't happen in football or any other stick-and-ball sport. But it can in NASCAR.

Our version would look like this: a dominant car has opened up a ten-second lead and then, after 499 miles, on the backstretch of the final lap, a part breaks, the car slows, and just like that, if the driver is lucky, he finishes fifteenth to twentieth place.

Such a scenario could send hundreds of thousands of dollars down the drain. What's worse is that the part that broke might have cost fifty dollars.

Too many times in our early years, parts and pieces that were out of our control cost us races. Because of this, we decided to control our destiny as much as possible. That decision started what turned out to be a twenty-five-year process during which we have evolved from being totally reliant on outside sources for car parts and pieces to making about 95 percent of what goes on and inside our cars in-house.

Becoming almost completely vertical on our cars meant making choices that cost us more time and more money, but all were necessary to stay on mission. Nothing is more diametrically opposed to a mission of going fast than unreliable parts. Gradually, over two and a half decades, we minimized the risk of working on a race car, hiring the best driver available to sit behind the wheel, developing a great strategy, and then seeing our day end with explaining to Toyota or FedEx or Mars that their car didn't win because a bracket we purchased from Bob's Bracket Shop broke.

When Coach started our team, nothing that went on or in our cars was original to our shop. All our parts and pieces came from suppliers with whom we had no involvement in their processes. We did not know the quality of the materials, who was putting the parts together, or the level of their quality control.

Hendrick Motorsports was one of NASCAR's giants when our team started (and it still is). The movie *Days of Thunder* was primarily based on HMS, which provided the cars for the movie's main driver characters. We bought Hendrick's old equipment to launch our team. Because of the high cost of building engines, a few anchor teams built all the engines for the cars of their specific manufacturers. Coach decided to lease engines until we established our team. Our engines for the first five seasons came from Hendrick.

Coach and Rick Hendrick were close friends, and HMS made good engines for us. When Bobby Labonte won three races for us in 1995, I'm sure Hendrick's drivers weren't pleased to see a driver from another team climbing out of a car in Victory Lane with a Hendrick-made engine under the hood.

But we knew that to become the best, we not only had to beat the best teams, but we also could not be dependent upon them in order to beat them. Imagine Coach calling the Dallas Cowboys' coach the week of a Redskins-Cowboys game and saying, "We sure could use a running back for the game." And even if he could, do you think the Cowboys would send over Emmitt Smith? No chance.

Coach decided that if we were going to compete with the big teams at the racetrack, we would have to make our own car parts and pieces. We created a CNC department to build parts we identified as ones we could make lighter, stronger, and more reliable than our vendors. We hired experts from the manufacturing industry who made our team better.

Exhibit A for making parts in-house was our constant struggle with the pit guns used to loosen and tighten lug nuts. Few things can gain or lose more positions during a race than a pit stop, and just as a broken part can sabotage a car from going fast, a bad air gun can cost a team valuable seconds and, perhaps, a race.

By this time, pit stops had become all about athletes. Early on, mechanics performed our pit stops. But then our sport started hiring athletes and training them to do the pit stops, making all our teams faster.

In typical JGR fashion, we went overboard in our pursuit of going fast. We built a weight room that rivaled Coach's in the NFL. We structured training and practices that included watching film—again, modeled after Coach's experience in the NFL. Pit crews were Todd Meredith's baby, and he was a phenomenal leader. Because of the training, the athletes got better and our pit stops got faster. Eventually the athletes became better than the equipment, to the point that the equipment was holding our teams back. A top tire changer, for example, could remove or put on five lug nuts in only one second. But our pit crew guys' hands had become quicker than the pit guns available from local vendors. Plus, the guns were unreliable.

Todd asked whether we could make our own guns. Enter Project SUB-12. At the time, a pit stop changing all four tires, filling the fuel tank, and making any needed adjustments to the car took about fourteen seconds. The name "SUB-12" came from the belief that with proper equipment, we could improve our pit stops to under twelve seconds.

The project started slow. We assigned an intern to it, and then another, and went through several iterations. The first custom pit gun exploded when we tested it. But, hey, blame it on the intern! We eventually got the pit gun right and designed and built every single component in-house. The gun was stronger, lighter, and smoother than previous guns. And, oh, was it faster. On the old vendor guns, the sockets spun at 8,000 revolutions per minute. Our last generation ran at 18,000 rpm.

We were the only team building guns, and word got out about "the Gibbs guns," partly because they were so loud that they stood out like a jet engine at a kite festival. Other teams were trying to take pictures of our guns. That first year, we protected them like the Holy Grail. We carried our pit guns to tracks in a locked container. During a race, each gun was covered with a towel right until the moment it was used and then immediately covered again.

Our pit stops dropped below twelve seconds. Then eleven. At our best, we were in the low tens. As our times dropped, the guns caused so much angst in the garage that they were banned in 2018, with NASCAR mandating teams go back to using one standard gun because, in their words, equipment should not give a team an advantage. That decision was disappointing, because our guns allowed our athletes to perform at their best. But as any good team does, we adapted to the new average guns and assigned our pit gun "scientist" to another build-it-better project.

The pit gun symbolizes how we do things at JGR: dream big, then outwork and outthink everyone. Control your own destiny—we've done so with hundreds of small things.

In addition to the short-lived pit guns, we have spent an inordinate amount of money and time enacting obsessive quality-control processes. We built a quality control department with microscopes, white lab coats—the whole thing. Regardless of whether a part was made by us or by an outside vendor, before the part goes on one of our race cars, we assume it has a flaw. When a batch of parts comes in, the mantra from Coach on down is "Assume every part that comes into the building is wrong—and don't change that assumption until you've thoroughly examined it." We select a random sample of each batch and check everything from weight, size, and structural integrity to ensure they are identical and perfect. When we order parts, we order multiple batches so we are not totally reliant on a single batch or vendor.

> The more a company controls its destiny, the more it increases accountability and eliminates excuses.

Our model is not the most cost-efficient. If we were mass-producing pieces to sell for profit, the model would look different. But our mission is going fast, and to stay on mission, every part that goes onto our cars needs to be perfect.

In order to go fast, we've had to eliminate excuses. Then if failure happens, we don't have to explain to a sponsor why their investment was dependent upon Bob's Bracket Shop or Gus's Transmissions. If something goes wrong with a car, we want to look our sponsors in the eyes and say, "This is on us. We'll get better."

And we have.

## Pain for Gain

An alliance with Hendrick Motorsports allowed us to get into racing. Now, as a large team, we are able to do the same for smaller teams by providing services and products in exchange for a negotiated alliance fee.

Alliances can serve the same purpose as sponsorships by bringing in additional revenue. They also provide another driver, crew chief, and team for exchanging feedback. Both help us go fast.

Based on our experience as a new team, I consider alliances a brilliant model. New and smaller teams can tap into our more than five hundred employees and almost thirty years of experience. They then can take our finished product and tweak it to their liking, putting them light-years ahead of doing everything from scratch.

Before the 2016 season, we entered into an alliance with Furniture Row Racing and its owner, Barney Visser. The alliance added a third benefit in that it was good for Toyota. We were Toyota's lead team, but NASCAR rules limit teams to four cars. Our alliance with Furniture Row provided Toyota a fifth team with one funnel of information through Joe Gibbs Racing.

I remember Todd Meredith saying, "Furniture Row is going to win a championship. They are good enough with our help that I think we need to prepare for that possibility." Todd was correct, because Martin Truex Jr. won the 2017 championship driving for Furniture Row.

In all honesty, as Martin's team celebrated its championship, I felt sick. I think all of us at JGR did. Our biggest partner, Toyota, had won a championship that we helped deliver, and I knew winning was great for them. We also had made good on our word not to hold anything back from Furniture Row. We said we would provide them the opportunity to beat us, and they did. But when Martin's car crossed the finish line, I threw my headset on the ground like a big baby because I felt like we had sold our souls.

We entered into the alliance because it helped us go fast, but the team we were assisting went faster than us. I could hear the first question from sponsors: "Let me get this straight: we lost the championship to a team you sold all your secrets to?"

Furniture Row folded after the next season, which provided us with an opportunity. Because of our familiarity with their team, we were able to bring in Martin and his crew chief, Cole Pearn, for our number 19 car. Plus, we took on their primary sponsor, Bass Pro Shops, to continue their partnership with Martin.

Of course, as happens regularly within this business, public perception of hiring Martin and Cole was not good. The criticism went something like this: "Alliance team beats larger teammate, goes out of business, larger teammate takes driver and sponsor. Yeah, sure." There was much more to the story than was publicly known, and Furniture Row's exit from the sport was outside of our control.

Bringing in Martin, Cole, and Bass Pro Shops in 2019 helped our team to our greatest season ever, with Martin claiming seven of our record-breaking nineteen victories. Ultimately, that alliance made our team better. But it did come with some pain.

Being part of an alliance also means releasing intellectual property. Intellectual property is the most treasured possession we have in our building. In our early days when Coach started signing team members to contracts, we probably never thought there would come a day when we would basically permit our intellectual property to leave for another team. We made the difficult decision to allow that in exchange for the alliance fee, because the alliance income helps us go fast. Going forward, we have to evaluate the risk/reward of offering our intellectual property. We have to determine, Does the gain justify the pain?

And, as always, we will stay on mission by answering that question in light of the most important question: Does this make us go fast?

## TOPICS FOR REFLECTION

1. Every organization needs a guiding compass that directs its decisions. Our "true north" is going fast. What is your organization's true north? What is your personal true north? How does that affect the way you make decisions every day?
2. Controlling our destiny in as many areas as possible helped us focus on our mission. In what ways does your organization control its own destiny? Are there opportunities to further control the process?

# Chapter 10

# PEOPLE FULFILL
# THE MISSION

OUR MISSION OF GOING FAST starts with people. Parts and tricks do not make us go fast by themselves. People do.

I have shared my belief about the importance of employees making themselves indispensable. In our business, the best way to do that is to make the car go fast. But many of our folks, including me, don't directly do that because we do not touch the car.

Typically, when we say someone makes us go fast, we are referring to employees who directly impact a car's performance—such as drivers, crew chiefs, pit crew members, engineers, those who work in R and D, and fabricators. But we have many people who directly contribute to the mission despite not having high-profile jobs. These folks make themselves indispensable in other ways. Consider Melissa and Paige, for example.

Melissa works our front desk and is excellent at her job. Coach often points out that Melissa holds one of the most important jobs at JGR. For the large majority of people who enter our building—probably 80 percent—Melissa is the only JGR employee they talk to. Their impression of their time on our company's property is built upon their impression of Melissa. Joe Gibbs Racing is the name of the company, Joe's name is on the building and shirts, but when most of our guests leave and tell someone, "I visited Joe Gibbs Racing, and they were so nice and let me take pictures," they're actually saying, "Melissa was so nice."

When someone calls our offices, hears the automated message, and needs to talk to a human, they talk to Paige. As with Melissa and our guests, when they receive a pleasant customer service experience—which they will receive from Paige—and then tell someone that "Joe Gibbs Racing was great because they helped me get what I needed," they're saying, "Paige helped me."

Melissa and Paige are each one person doing a job that represents the entire company. Coach considers them valuable players who help us go fast indirectly because of how competently they handle our loyal fans and customers.

Robin was here on day one, even before the three musketeers. Robin has basically held the front office together for JGR's entire existence, but most people outside of our building do not know her name. Coach talks about his favorite role players from his football days—guys who were unknown to many fans but who held the team together. In many ways, Robin has been the glue that has defined our culture and kept us focused on our mission. Robin has a quiet, gentle spirit with a servant's heart as she organizes events for employee spouses, plans the Christmas party, and mobilizes volunteer teams in the community. She doesn't touch the race cars, but I would argue that she has played a role in every victory because we don't win with parts and pieces—we win with people.

One of my favorite examples of how someone can indirectly play a role in fulfilling our mission is a former custodian named Larry.

Larry was a semiretired, former military member we hired as a janitor. I had exchanged pleasantries with Larry whenever we crossed paths, but rarely more than a sentence or two—a "good night" on my way out of the office or "this looks great" when he was cleaning a restroom counter.

One day I entered a restroom that Larry was preparing to clean.

"Sorry," I said and turned around to go to another restroom.

"No, no," he said. "Go ahead. I'll get started after you're done."

As I made small talk with Larry, I pointed to the headphones he was wearing.

"What are you listening to?" I asked.

"I'm listening to a biography on Abraham Lincoln," he replied.

"Really?"

"Yes, sir. I'm fascinated by presidents. I have an audiobook on all of them, and I'm going through them in order to learn more about them."

"What else do you listen to?" I asked.

He rattled off a list of books he had listened to, all classics with intriguing topics.

From that day forward, I made a point to ask Larry on my way out each evening to share one nugget with me that he had learned that day. He possessed a wealth of knowledge.

Larry was such a happy, articulate man, and through a series of conversations, I learned that he had fought in a war, returned home, and started working in corporate America. But he had grown tired of the rat race and wanted a job that would allow him to maximize his time to learn about US presidents and whatever else he wanted to discover.

To be completely honest, Larry did not fit my expectations of someone we would hire as a custodian. But I grew to envy Larry. He was getting paid to learn all day. I could envision Larry getting into his car after work every day, smarter and with his workday behind him. No texts, no angry clients or drivers, no late-night calls from Coach! He could go home to his family in peace.

Larry had life figured out much more than many of us do. He taught me why it's important to engage with people at work whom you see but don't typically talk with. It's so easy to bury our heads in our phones or rush down the hall to our next meeting or look down without making eye contact with the person with whom we're sharing an elevator ride.

Outside the office, we can get so caught up in our business conversations that we fail to recognize the waiter is a person who has a story that might surprise us. All around us are opportunities to give a little bit of ourselves away if we will just be mindful of engaging with others. And as I found out with Larry, they will often teach us something.

Indirectly, Larry helped us go fast. He came to work every day, kept the place clean, didn't care about his title, and showed a good attitude as he shared an encouraging word with those walking past him in the hallway. Without doubt, Larry performed his job with excellence and added to our culture by caring about his job. Employees like Larry are contagious culture boosters, and culture is the engine that powers the mission.

I've heard a story about a janitor for NASA in the 1960s who was asked, "What do you do for NASA?" His reply was, "I'm helping put a man on the moon." He had bought in to being part of the mission.

Larry retired in 2015, and I would bet if someone asks him what he did for JGR, he would answer, "I helped them go fast." And he would be correct.

> "Role players" become more connected to their company's mission when the leaders become personally connected to the role players.

## The Expendable Carpet-Walker

The reason I am so aware of the people who don't directly make us go fast is that I have been one my entire career. I used to say, "Either you make the car go fast, or you're expendable." I guess I have been Exhibit A for "expendable" my entire career.

Granted, Coach would express a different opinion, even back to my days as the T-shirt and licensing guy. He insisted that my work helped fund our car and, thus, was important to the mission. He had a gift for making me truly believe I helped us go fast—a trait of a great leader.

Today, he would say that all employees who take care of sponsors or customers are indirectly contributing to our mission because they are feeding the machine downstairs that is making our cars go fast. And he wants buy-in on that from custodian to president, because if we aren't all fulfilling the mission, none of us has a job. This is true no matter anyone's role in any company, but I understand that sometimes it's difficult for everyone to see themselves as mission critical.

No matter how much Coach has sold me on my importance and role in our mission, I have always had a complex about being expendable. For my first twenty years, I did not have an employment contract. Being J.D.'s buddy, I guess Coach figured we had a blood oath that I would never leave. But not having a contract added to my complex of feeling expendable. It didn't help that for those first twenty years, I absorbed an onslaught of "carpet-walker" wisecracks from the guys who knew they made our cars go fast.

When I arrived at the racetrack almost every week, at least one of the guys would ask, "What are you doing here?" I usually tried to answer with humor, like "I'm on vacation" or "I came to see you." But the question bothered me. I thought they were serious. I was J.D.'s friend and often felt that people thought I was coasting because of my connection to him. That perception fueled me in many ways.

I arrived at the racetrack each week with a complex about being in the way, because the car guys had ingrained in my head that I was a front-office guy, and unless I was wearing a uniform like them, I didn't belong at the track. We laugh about that now, but it took me about two decades to move beyond that feeling. (Although even now, as I entertain clients during race weekends, I still feel like I'm in the way when I'm in the pits or the garage. After all, as president and as an ambassador to our clients, I attend races to socialize. Somebody has to do it!)

I can, however, with 100-percent certainty point to a moment when everyone at Joe Gibbs Racing knew I was not contributing to making us go fast.

There is no time during a race when a carpet-walker feels more in the way than during a pit stop.

One of the most intriguing aspects of NASCAR is the access. In the NFL, no fan or sponsor can stand right behind the head coach on the sideline during a game. But that happens every weekend in NASCAR.

We bring sponsors to races, and the top executives usually stand in the pits (our sidelines) and experience that unique perspective on a race. Some sit on the pit box, which is the command center down on pit road where the crew chief, team owner, and other important members of the team sit to make the necessary decisions during a race. Our guests are able to look over their shoulders to see all the data the crew chief and company are monitoring.

Our guests also wear headsets that allow them to listen in on the in-race conversations between the crew chief, driver, and spotter. I have often said that if other pro sports were live-miked, they would lose all their corporate sponsors. That's not a knock; it's just human nature that athletes can use some rough language in the heat of battle. Ours are held to a higher standard, but they are still human. Sometimes our guests hear a driver's tirade that makes me cringe, but they enjoy being able to hear what's taking place in real time. We have the greatest access in all of pro sports.

I wander from pit to pit during races, and one of the coolest sights is the tire changers staying prepped for a pit stop by loosening and tightening lug nuts on a practice wheel. The way those guys can loosen or tighten all five lug nuts on a wheel in one second is amazing. But for the majority of a race, the pit crew members are spectators who didn't have to purchase a ticket. Because the only part of the track that is usually visible from the pits is the straightaway in front of pit road, the best way for the crew to keep up with a race, other than the team communications, is to watch the race on the track's big screen or on TV monitors in the pit. It's not uncommon to see at least one crew member sitting on the pit wall, back to the straightaway as cars speed past behind him while he watches the race on TV. But once the call for a pit stop is made, the pit becomes a flurry of activity.

Back in 1996 or 1997, when we still were in our one-car days, I was entertaining sponsors at Charlotte Motor Speedway.

At one point during the race, Bobby Labonte needed to come in for an unscheduled pit stop. When the call came in over the radio, the guy who gives Bobby a new water bottle just so happened to be making an unscheduled pit stop of his own.

As the crew members sprang into their positions, someone noticed the absence of the water bottle guy, and guess who got tapped to take over? Yes, the carpet-walker.

Fortunately, I had only thirty seconds to stress over my new job—although they were a *very long* thirty seconds. If they had given me more notice, I probably would have sprinted to the porta potty and yanked our water bottle guy out so I could step in and throw up.

NASCAR rules limit the number of crew members who go over the wall during a pit stop. With four tires to change, a jack needed to lift the car, and fuel to add to the tank—hopefully in less than twelve seconds—the water bottle guy isn't going to make the over-the-wall list. Instead, he gets the water bottle to the driver via a long metal pole.

In a situation where highly trained professionals move with Swiss-watch-like precision and every tenth of a second counts, my on-the-job training consisted entirely of being handed a filled bottle and pointed toward the water bottle pole on the ground. In what can only be described as a testimony to how well God wired the human brain, I spent those thirty seconds imagining every possible scenario that could take place during the pit stop, estimating how much the pole would bend with the full bottle on the end, and calculating how much to compensate for the wind.

As Bobby neared the pit, I stretched the pole out high enough that it wouldn't bonk any of our over-the-wall guys on the head. When the car screeched to a stop, the tire and jack guys dashed to the far side of the car, and I lowered the pole and perfectly navigated the most difficult part of the job—inserting the end with the water bottle into the six-inch-wide opening beside the driver's window safety net. Then the one scenario I had not contemplated occurred. Bobby waved off the water bottle. I guess because he had come into the pits earlier than planned, he didn't need more water yet. Still, I hadn't planned on Bobby not removing the water bottle and keeping it in his car.

Caught off guard, I pulled the pole back, and the bottle snagged on the edge of the window net, came off the pole, and fell to the ground. With the jackman rounding the front left corner of the car to lift the near side, I watched helplessly as the bottle continued to roll until it wedged itself under the side of the car at the exact spot where the jack-man would insert the jack so he could raise the car for the tire-changers.

I gasped.

Fortunately, the bottle's presence did not deter the jackman, who crammed the jack into its spot, forcing the bottle underneath the car and out of sight.

In a matter of seconds, the tire-changers changed out the left-side tires, the fuel man finished filling the tank, and the jack man lowered the jack and pulled it out from underneath the car. Bobby spun his tires to exit the pit, and I breathed a sigh of relief that my screwup hadn't ruined the stop. At that precise moment, I discovered where the jack had sent the water bottle. There it was, wedged against the front of the right rear tire.

As Bobby peeled out, the tire crushed the bottle and sent it soaring backward, fifty yards down pit road, a stream of water and ice cubes following it like a comet's tail. The flying bottle caught the attention of not only our own pit crew but also the crews in the pit stalls behind us. As if choreographed, every single team member standing in our pit and sitting in our pit box turned at the exact same time and stared at me, standing there holding the now-empty pole like an idiot. That included Jimmy Makar, who still was "Mad Dog" at the time.

I sheepishly lowered my chin, laid down the pole, and walked out the back of the pit. Words cannot describe how much I wished JGR would have been a multicar team back then so I could have skulked off to a different pit. But back then, Bobby was it for us. I had nowhere to hide.

No one yelled at me. I wished they would have. Instead, they just glared at me, shook their heads in a way that seemed to confirm their suspicions that I was an expendable idiot who would screw up even the easiest of tasks, and went back to their business of trying to make our car go fast. That was more than two decades ago, and it was the last time I have been asked to help the car guys during a race.

Sometimes, I learned, keeping the team on mission means rolling up your sleeves, and other times it means staying out of the way. We all play a part in the mission. But we can't play every part.

## TOPICS FOR REFLECTION

1. People are crucial because they help fulfill the mission. At JGR, even people who don't touch the cars (like me) are critical to the mission of helping our cars go fast. Think about your role in your organization. How does your role contribute to the overall mission of the organization? How are you, like that janitor for NASA, "helping put a man on the moon"?

2. What percentage of the time do you feel like your tasks are mission critical versus feeling like they are insignificant or disconnected from your organization's overall mission? Why do you feel that way? Are there steps you can take to shift your mindset?

## Chapter 11

# A MISSION-CRITICAL PARTNER

No INDUSTRY IS MORE VITAL to the health of NASCAR than the automotive industry. While sponsors come and go, car companies remain the foundation of our sport. The adage "Win on Sunday, sell on Monday" is 100 percent alive and well in this business for Toyota, Ford, and Chevy.

For our first sixteen seasons, we raced for General Motors and enjoyed a great deal of success, including winning three championships in Pontiacs and Chevrolets. The GM folks were great, and we will always be grateful to them for helping us get started in the sport and for their many years of support.

In our partnership with GM, regardless of how successful we were, we would always be a small fish in a big pond. Other anchor Chevy teams had existed longer than us and had earned a higher spot on the totem pole. In terms of support, we saw little room to grow.

In 2007, Toyota entered the NASCAR Cup Series as a new manufacturer. Toyota's approach was different. While Ford and Chevy supported a large number of organizations, Toyota set out to focus on a much tighter group, intent on fielding a smaller number of very high-performing cars. Toyota's strategy prioritized quality over quantity. Additionally, unlike the other car manufacturers, Toyota desired to become a part of the process by embedding people inside an organization. They also planned to conduct independent research and projects in their own facility and even provide engines for their teams.

Toyota's model was completely different, and when they expressed interest in talking with us during the 2007 season, we jumped at the opportunity.

From the first meeting, Toyota's mission was so clearly aligned with JGR's that it almost seemed uncanny. Like us, they demonstrated an uncompromising passion for and pursuit of going fast. Our corporate cultures were a perfect match; we felt like Toyota and JGR were made for each other.

Toyota had not won a race in its first year in the Cup Series, but it had established the foundation by assembling all the pieces it needed through its racing arm, Toyota Racing Development (TRD). We anticipated growing pains if we changed manufacturers, but the vote was unanimous—albeit with slight reservations—to move to Toyota for the 2008 season.

That might be the single best decision our company has ever made. We won ten races in our first season with Toyota, and we have maintained that average every season since—by far the best in our sport.

Toyota's and JGR's secret sauces come from similar recipes. Toyota's people are as competitive and committed to winning as our people, a key ingredient in a great partnership.

The executives at Toyota corporate—Bob Carter and his team: Jack Hollis, Bill Fay, Ed Laukes, Vinay Shahani, Isaka Kanazawa, and Paul Doleshal—have become family to us. The racing guys—TRD president David Wilson and Tyler Gibbs (no relation to Coach)—are literally part of our team. I have so much respect for them that I find more joy in winning because of what it means to them than for what it means to me.

When we drive a Toyota Camry into Victory Lane, we are helping Toyota dealerships across America sell cars. (Our family has four Toyotas in the driveway.) I would like to think that our thirteen years of winning with Toyota have had something to do with the Camry being the best-selling car in America all thirteen of those years.

## Prepare . . . and Be Flexible

Part of staying on mission is always being prepared. Yet no matter how confident you are in your plans, always be flexible.

As a planner, I try to look at every possible scenario in my life and in business. That's how I am wired. My family calls these scenarios I consider "Dave's plans." But often in business, as in life, all the "Dave's plans" in the world don't matter.

During the 2016 season, we won twelve races, with four by Kyle Busch, three each by Carl Edwards and Denny Hamlin, and two by Matt Kenseth. All four made it to the Round of 8 in the Cup playoffs, and Kyle and Carl qualified for the Championship 4. In the championship race, the Ford EcoBoost 400 at Homestead, Carl dominated the race and led with ten laps to go when a caution flag came out. I was confident going into the restart that Carl and Kyle would finish first and second, and with Kyle's 2015 title, we were on the verge of winning the championship for a second consecutive year.

Instead, Carl had a devastating crash that ended his title hopes. Little did we know that race would be the end of his career.

A few weeks later, Carl called Coach and said he wanted to come by to see us. I assumed that with the Christmas break coming up, he wanted to express his thanks for a great season in person and wish people a merry Christmas, because that's the kind of thoughtful guy Carl is.

Carl came into our office and dropped a bomb.

"I've been thinking about it a lot," he said. "I'm retiring."

We thought he was kidding. Carl was thirty-seven, had a year remaining on his contract, and, in my opinion, was at the peak of his career.

Coach reminded Carl of what he frequently tells our drivers, that they have a job that millions of people around the world dream of having. Carl explained that he was content with what he had accomplished in his career, he wanted to pursue a few non-racing interests, and he was not taking lightly his opportunity to leave our sport fully healthy.

Surprised would be a gross understatement to describe our reaction. To quote Chevy Chase from *Christmas Vacation*, "If I woke up tomorrow with my head sewn to the carpet, I wouldn't be more surprised than I am right now."

Because of the monumental ramifications of such a decision, Coach suggested that Carl take a few more days to think. Four days later, Carl called and said he was certain he wanted to walk away from the sport.

The week before Carl had come in to talk with us, our executive team had written out fifteen different contingencies we anticipated could happen over the next three years. Carl retiring with a year left on his contract was not one of them. Goodbye, Dave's plans.

Following Carl's decision, we gathered and decided to promote Daniel Suárez into Carl's number 19 car. Daniel was a promising young driver who had won the Xfinity Series championship the same weekend that Carl had come up short in his bid for the Cup championship. That title made him the first Mexican-born driver to win a NASCAR championship. We had projected giving Daniel at least one more year to develop below the Cup level, but our timeline accelerated with Carl's decision.

If only the fallout had been limited to replacing Carl.

One driver's retirement can affect hundreds of people. With a superstar driver retiring with one year left on his contract, sponsors could have told us they wanted out of their deals with us. It's no exaggeration to say that we could have been forced to shut down a team. The long list of unanswered questions brought in a time of uncertainty for many people—and it was the week of Christmas.

The day after Carl confirmed he would retire, several of us flew to different parts of the country for important conversations. Most of our corporate partners tied in with Carl were preparing to take time off for Christmas. Instead, we were asking to meet with their executives. I met with one CEO the day before Christmas Eve.

Almost every one of the conversations started with, "You're not going to believe this one." Then we informed them that Carl was retiring and Daniel was taking his place.

Fortunately, all our sponsors were gracious with us. But just as a brand sponsoring Tiger Woods would not pay the same for a rookie golfer, a sponsor paying for Carl Edwards would not pay the same for a young, unproven driver. Because all the sponsor contracts were pegged to Carl having one year left on his deal, the contracts had to be amended and then rushed through approval processes with lawyers. The rare break Christmas brings immediately evaporated for a lot of folks at JGR as they dealt with sponsor details, new contracts, car and testing preparations for a rookie driver, and future sponsorship projections. I felt like I had a phone attached to my ear all day every day, and several others were on the phone more than me.

That experience made me wonder, *Why do we even make plans?* I mean, we thought we were prepared for anything, but the unexpected happened and blew up all our plans. Of course, that one story does not reflect all the times our plans *did* have us prepared for what could have been unexpected changes. Every good team needs to be prepared for the unexpected.

## From Plan B to Championship
In May 2007, four months into the Cup season, Dale Earnhardt Jr. announced that he would seek a new team to join for 2008. Dale Junior

had driven in the Cup series only for Dale Earnhardt Inc., the team his father had founded in 1980, five years before the elder Earnhardt's fatal crash at the Daytona 500.

Junior's pending departure set off a feeding frenzy among all the teams. I don't know if there has been a more high-profile driver in NASCAR history to become, essentially, a free agent. It was NASCAR's version of the LeBron James free agency, with everyone speculating to which team Junior would take his talents. At that time, Dale had won NASCAR's most popular driver award four consecutive years. (He won the award every season after that until his retirement in 2017, a total of fifteen consecutive years.)

Bobby Labonte was no longer in the number 18 car, and the team had struggled since Bobby's departure. The timing was perfect for putting Dale in that car, and he seemed like a great fit to us. So we entered the recruiting race.

JGR had grown to the point that we had a late shift of about eight employees building parts in the machine shop. To bring Dale in covertly, we told our facilities manager to figure out a way to empty the building on the night of Dale's visit. Our facilities manager scheduled electricity maintenance for that night and emailed everyone to vacate the building by seven o'clock.

Dale and Kelley, his sister and business manager, arrived around 10 p.m. Dale had long been public with his love of the Washington Redskins, and when Coach and Dale shook hands, Dale said, "It's an honor to be here, Coach." We felt the same about having Dale in our shop.

After a walk around our building, we sat in Coach's office to talk. Dale's first question was direct: "So, what's wrong with the 18 car?"

Without hesitating, Coach replied, "Nothing. That's why you're here."

We talked for a couple of hours about JGR's history, our culture, and why we believed Dale needed to drive for us. I felt like we developed a quick chemistry with Dale, and when he and Kelley left, I thought we had a shot at landing him.

Back in the office the next day, we started planning the next meeting with the Earnhardts, when we would discuss contract numbers and extras we could package to sweeten a deal with us.

Coach was in his second go-round with the Redskins, and the next week, Redskins owner Dan Snyder offered his team's jet to bring in Dale and Kelley for a return visit with us in DC. J.D. and I flew to DC with Junior and Kelley. We talked Redskins and politics the entire flight. Junior impressed me as smart and engaging. Upon our arrival in DC, a private helicopter took the four of us to land in Mr. Snyder's backyard. That was probably the highlight of my career to that point.

Inside Mr. Snyder's home, we made what I considered the best sales pitch we had delivered to anyone. Here Dale was with the Hall of Fame coach in the home of the owner of his favorite NFL team. I was giddy with optimism. Coach wanted to close the deal in that meeting, and we had a check for Dale's signing bonus ready to hand him. Dale was gracious but not ready to commit, and J.D. and I flew with him and Kelley back to North Carolina.

After we dropped off Dale and Kelley, J.D. and I called Coach. J.D. and I were so confident with our pitch to Dale that we were high-fiving each other as we reported our conversations with Dale and Kelley on the plane.

My annual bonus at the time revolved around merchandise sales, and Dale was the king of NASCAR merchandising. I envisioned all the opportunities I could pursue with the sport's most popular driver on our team. Plus, I really liked Junior personally. I was more excited than I had been up to that point in my career, and, selfishly, I saw a chance to put myself on the map selling his merchandise.

We considered ourselves the front-runner for Dale and believed Hendrick Motorsports to be our biggest competitor. Hendrick was

NASCAR's dynasty team, but owner Rick Hendrick masterfully responded to a media question about pursuing Dale by answering, "There's no room at the inn here." The strategy worked, because with Hendrick apparently saying he didn't have room for a new driver, there was little speculation of HMS being in the chase for Dale.

That abruptly ended one night about two weeks after our meeting with Dale. He called and cordially said, "Listen, guys. You made this really hard for me. But we've made the decision to go somewhere else." The next morning, word broke of a press conference at Hendrick's head-quarters to announce the signing of Dale.

That phone call was a moment of sheer devastation for all of us. A real gut punch.

Bill France Jr., the son of NASCAR's founder and a longtime CEO of our sport, had died that same week. I was still mad about losing out on Junior when we boarded the plane to attend Mr. France's funeral. Coach was in a much better mood than me because he was rational and accepting of what had occurred.

Rick was one of the speakers at the funeral, and having just learned that he was getting Dale, I didn't have Rick high on my list of favorites that day. But Rick, with his winsome manner, was so articulate and gracious as he spoke that, three minutes into his speech, I was thinking, *Wow—what a great guy!* I actually felt some peace, like Dale had ended up in a good place.

When HMS signed Dale, the company announced that he would replace Kyle Busch, a young and brash driver with crazy-good talent and questions about whether his attitude could fit into a team.

We set up a meeting with Kyle. I was still angry about losing Junior, and Kyle was no Junior from a merchandise standpoint. My impression of Kyle also was not positive.

But in our meeting, Kyle presented himself differently than I had anticipated. He was smart, funny, and said all the things we wanted to hear from our next potential driver. His mission aligned with ours:

"Go fast on every lap." I knew Kyle only by reputation before our meeting, but I walked out understanding that the bottom line with Kyle was that he wanted to win as much as any driver I had met. I could see how some of the knock on Kyle came from his intense desire to win.

We signed Kyle to fill the number 18 in 2008, and in his first season with us he won eight races. He's still part of our team, of course, and he has driven his way into the conversation for greatest driver in NASCAR history.

My wife says there are times when what appears to be rejection actually is the Lord's protection. I would have loved to sign Dale and will forever wonder how life would have looked for us had we done so. I will always be a fan of Junior and respect how he represented our sport throughout his career. But our plan B of getting Kyle when we didn't sign Dale turned out to be one of the best moves in our team's history.

> What appears to us to be rejection often is the Lord's protection.

We had a plan to sign Dale. We made our best presentation and forged a chemistry with Junior unlike we'd experienced during any other recruiting visit. On paper, everything was perfect. But when Dale rejected our offer, we had to be flexible to wipe away the disappointment—one of us, ahem, was slower to do that than the others—and move quickly to put together a new plan. What was meant to be came to pass, and I learned amazing life lessons through the process.

### "Big Brands Do Big Things"
We announced our signing of Kyle in August 2007, complete with a Redskins number 18 jersey to honor our prized free-agent addition.

Around that time, Mars and the M&M'S brand decided to shop around NASCAR in search of a new team.

NASCAR sponsors come one of two ways—either a new sponsor joining the sport (like FedEx) or one that has been around but is looking for a fresh start. Mars fit the latter category. When we met with Mars executives, they informed us that they were meeting with all the top teams. That's a strategy I highly recommend to sponsors.

Racing provides a marketing platform for a brand. Each brand has a unique set of objectives it wants to accomplish through racing, and the objectives are different for every company. FedEx wanted shipping business from other companies. Home Depot aimed to build employee morale. Interstate Batteries wanted to build its brand.

I believe that sponsors should talk with as many teams as possible to find the best fit for meeting their objectives. Cultures need to match. A team needs to demonstrate a record of providing a company's key deliverables. Because I consider us to be a Nordstrom of race teams with our superior product and exceptional service, we are not a low-cost provider. If a brand fits better with another team, that's okay. Our sport needs forty healthy, sponsored cars each weekend, and the more Fortune 500-type brands in NASCAR, the better we all are.

William Clements, the longtime marketing guru at Mars who oversees its racing program, made a comment in our meeting that I will always remember: "Big brands do big things." William attributed the quote to Forrest Mars Sr., one of the company's founders.

Mars had been in our sport for over a decade and had won only a handful of races. If the company stayed in racing, it wanted to partner with a big name for big results. After all, the world's number-one candy brand deserved a number-one-caliber driver.

Our good friends at Interstate Batteries had sponsored the 18 car from our start and were all-in on racing. But after sixteen seasons, Interstate was willing to give up a chunk of the races as primary sponsor to another company while also expanding into each of our other cars to embrace a "family of drivers" approach. We pitched Mars sponsorship of thirty races with Kyle, a twenty-two-year-old relative newcomer to the Cup Series with three victories and a reputation of being a hothead. For a brand whose target demographic was moms at the grocery store, the potential match didn't seem perfect. Then add in the fact that we were switching to Toyota the following season, which brought uncertainty as to how long it would take us to adapt to the change in manufacturers.

But Mars wanted to go big and viewed Kyle as a champion in the making. Kyle's first meeting with Mars, as with his initial meeting with us, revealed a super-competitive guy who had more to him than expected. Mars made the decision to pair with Kyle, and that duo has become one of the most iconic sponsor-driver pairings in NASCAR history. Kyle won eight races in their first season together.

After the limited success Mars had experienced in NASCAR, seeing the reactions of the company, including the wonderful family that runs it, was priceless. Following one win, I was walking to Victory Lane with Brice Russell, a key executive at Mars who now serves on our advisory board. Brice told me, "We don't even know where Victory Lane is at this place."

Starting with 2008, no sponsor-driver combination has won more Cup races or led more laps than Mars and Kyle. Throw in the two Cup championships, and Mars truly has managed to do big things in NASCAR.

The 2008 season was special for us because we also were giving Toyota its first wins.

A year that started out with the disappointment of not landing Dale Jr. ended up producing not only Kyle but also Mars and Toyota—along with Interstate Batteries and FedEx, the Mount Rushmore of our racing partners.

Once again, God was faithful to Joe Gibbs Racing.

## TOPICS FOR REFLECTION

1. I place such a high value on making plans that my family and coworkers call my anticipating contingencies "Dave's plans." Yet, as I outlined in this chapter, it's not possible to plan for every potential situation. Are you a planner? What does "expect the unexpected" look like for you?

2. On a scale of 1 to 10, how flexible are you when plans change? If you rated yourself lower than a 7, why did you do so? How would you benefit if you were more flexible? How would your organization benefit?

## Chapter 12

# THE LAST PLANE OUT
# OF VIETNAM

MOST GREAT LEADERS HAVE AN INNATE SENSE of urgency about them. With Coach, urgency is on another level. I often say that his sense of urgency probably is the single biggest reason we are successful as an organization.

Coach treats every crisis, every task, every meeting like it's the last plane out of Vietnam.

As a football coach, he had a designated enemy each week. He had film on his upcoming opponent to study and had to devise a game plan to beat them, and he had a finite, predictable time frame within which to create that plan. In racing, Coach wants to win every race, but he isn't the tactician. And the race is only part of the battle for him. Recruiting a driver, obtaining a sponsor, resolving a personnel issue, or lobbying NASCAR not to change a rule are examples of common battles Coach takes on. He always needs at least one! If Coach doesn't have a battle in front of him, he's almost miserable.

In a given week, Coach could have a dozen people trying to hand him that one thing that is his battle. My role is to filter through the possibilities and help determine what should be his 9-1-1.

Coach is always on the move, so placing a battle in front of him is almost like those videos of cats chasing a laser pointer flashed onto a wall or a floor. Because of Coach's influence, we need his energy focused on tasks only he can accomplish. Once Coach has his assignment, he attacks with a dogged sense of urgency. He will not rest until the issue is resolved. (Truth be told, some of us around him won't rest until then either.) Then he's ready for his next issue.

One night, my phone rang at eleven o'clock. I was in bed and almost asleep, and when I saw the call was from Coach, I answered. Receiving a call from Coach at night is not unusual. It's funny, because his calls never start with, "Hey, how's it going?" or "Hey, Dave, is this a good time?" He always jumps directly into the issue at hand.

Coach had attended a sponsor's event that night and was preparing to board the plane to return home. When I answered, he started right in with a concern he had about the sponsor.

"Can you gather the group together at the office?" he asked.

The group was our executive team, and I knew he was implying that he wanted all of us to be in the conference room when he arrived at the office.

I looked at the clock. Coach's flight would last about an hour. Fortunately for me at that time of night, the math was simple. He would get to the office after midnight.

"Coach," I said. "I can do that. But let me ask you, is whatever it is that's going on still going to be an issue at, say, seven o'clock in the morning? Could we meet first thing tomorrow?"

Coach was silent for a moment. I could almost hear him thinking.

"Yeah, yeah, we can do that," he said. "Just get everybody to meet at seven. Thanks, Dave."

It never crossed his mind that waiting a few hours was an option. When we met the next morning, we discovered that the issue was one we had met about several times already and one for which Coach needed clarification and closure.

Urgency also can mean discussing the same topic multiple times. We laugh about it, but Coach's sense of urgency causes us to rethink and consider every possible solution when we have a problem. Just as he labored over football game plans so as not to miss any detail, we labor over big decisions and contemplate every possible outcome—usually many times.

That's the urgency with which Coach treats basically everything in our company, and his mindset permeates the building. For those of us in his first circle, and I would add even for managers, there's a feeling that if Coach has that sense of urgency, then we need to have it too. Coach values the opinion of those around him. Sometimes too much. I joke that Coach often manages by proximity. In other words, whoever happens to be closest to him when a situation comes up becomes his wingman.

> A leader's sense of urgency—or lack thereof—
> is reflected at every level of an organization.

I am a strategist and a planner. My number one trait according to CliftonStrengths is "strategic." From watching Coach, I have learned how to better deal with my stress, because as a strategist and a planner, I thrive most within structure. Coach has caused me to deal with surprises and spontaneous meetings.

Surprises are not my friends, and I don't like interruptions. Sometimes I feel like I have placed my entire life on an always-full calendar. I like to plan out my day much like a flight plan for a trip. I have an itinerary, and everything fits around the different places I need to be. I have a specific end point in mind, and I set my course for the day to reach that end point.

As a member of Coach's first circle, his sense of urgency affects me.

When something becomes critical to him, my schedule can be wrecked in a heartbeat. If I start a day hyperscheduled and have no margin, I know chaos will ensue for me. I do not claim to be great at this, but I have learned to accommodate Coach by scheduling margin into my day because I realize the unexpected needs to be expected.

In the early days of our company, nothing was more urgent for me than what Coach wanted. But as my responsibilities grew, and especially now as president, I have had to learn when to push back and how to prioritize where my own sense of urgency should be. Part of leading is "leading up"—the idea that we have to help manage those who manage us. If there is another meeting that day for which I will add the most value by attending, then I need to make that my priority.

I must consider where my time is best utilized in any situation. My question for determining my priorities is, Where will my time be most efficient for Joe Gibbs Racing? I need to identify the tasks that only I can do.

Just as with Coach allowing me to tap the brakes on that midnight meeting, Coach listens to me on what I consider my priorities to be because of two important elements of our relationship: trust and communication.

If I tell Coach something is more important for me to stay engaged with at that moment, he trusts the call I make. We both have unique relationships with sponsors and partners that require our individual attention, and we understand those dynamics and maintain mutual trust for each other's decisions.

Straightforward, honest dialogue is crucial to understanding and navigating each other's points of view and positions. Typically, that means face-to-face discussions to make sure we are moving in the same direction. Rarely does a text adequately communicate why I have something else that is more urgent than Coach's battle of the moment.

Coach and I have developed those elements of trust and communication over time, and they are vital to operating efficiently as a company.

## Making the Mission Evident

I believe one of the top reasons that drivers, crew chiefs, engineers, and people in other positions want to work for us is our mission of going fast. They see it on the racetrack, but it is even more evident during a visit to our shop.

Matt Kenseth raced for us from 2013 to 2017 in the number 20 car. When we recruited Matt, he came in for a late-night tour and meeting, as we did when we were pursuing Dale Earnhardt Jr. We learned early that the best time to walk a high-profile driver through our race shop is late at night. I think our janitor has more information than anyone else concerning the drivers we recruit. He has been sworn to secrecy numerous times.

Matt is stoic but has a very dry sense of humor. Throughout the hour-and-a-half tour, Matt was stone-faced. With him hiding his emotions, we had no clue what he was thinking. He also said little, instead choosing to listen intently to everything we said.

After Matt had toured the building and met with some of our technical guys, I was part of the group that met with him in our conference room. He had just looked behind the curtain at how we were set up, including the hundreds of little extra things we do that demonstrate our total commitment to going fast.

I asked Matt, "What do you think?"

He responded, "I don't know how anyone else ever wins a race."

Then we gave Matt our best sales pitch, and Matt opened up to ask a lot of good questions that showed he's a smart driver and an all-around smart guy.

After Matt left, Coach seemed uneasy.

"That went really bad," Coach said.

"What do you mean?" I asked.

"Yeah, that was awful," Coach continued. "We have no shot with him."

"No, no, no," one of our engineers said. "I think it went really well."

"How do you figure?" Coach asked.

"That's just Matt," the engineer said. "He just didn't want to look *too* interested. Joe, I actually think it went really well."

The room was split on whether we would be able to sign Matt. He did sign up with us, and what an awesome run it was. Although it has been almost a decade since Matt toured our facility, I still think often of his words: "I don't know how anyone else ever wins a race." That was an incredible compliment to our team, because he made that statement based on how he perceived our commitment to staying on mission.

While it would be easy to puff out our chest over a comment like Matt's, the truth is that we are trying to survive in a tough business. Our number one goal from a business standpoint is to stay on mission in everything we do. The minute we stop going fast, none of our other corporate goals will matter, because we will be out of business.

## Stay Humble, Stay Hungry

Joe Gibbs Racing has a zero-tolerance policy in regard to complacency. Coach won't allow us to become too satisfied with our accomplishments. The sense of urgency he has instilled in our company is reflected in a saying he often reminds us that he told his football players: "You need to be two things: humble and hungry. All the time. Stay humble, stay hungry. The hardest year to win is the year after you win a Super Bowl."

As the winner of three Super Bowls, Coach speaks from experience. That's why he is so against allowing complacency to sneak into our teams.

Humility and hunger are attitudes. They're choices.

J.D. is my best example of humility. Keep your mouth shut when you win. Don't talk about being great; just be great. He modeled those ideas in everything he did.

Remaining hungry is important because if we aren't hungry, we aren't going to push, we aren't going to be driven, and we will lose our sense of urgency.

One season's victories can become the next season's losses, with no apparent explanation for the difference. We have done a good job through the years of not allowing complacency to enter our culture following successful seasons. We've never sat back and celebrated so much that we fell behind the next season. Every team in NASCAR is constantly chasing success the same as us.

But sometimes, I fear we have done *too* good of a job of not becoming complacent—to the point that we don't enjoy our successes enough. Our constant pushing can make winning at times feel more like relief than a cause for celebration. This is probably the "feeler" in me coming through, but I've had to make a priority of learning to celebrate more—without losing the hunger to keep chasing success.

In 2015 on the night Kyle won the season championship, Coach, Todd, and I were sitting in Victory Lane at Homestead-Miami. It was forty-five minutes after the race had ended, and we still had confetti and champagne all over our clothes. We started talking about our Monday morning meeting, and with his last-plane-out-of-Vietnam intensity, Coach gave us a few 9-1-1 agenda items to discuss.

"Whoa, whoa, whoa," I said. "Can we just stop for a second? Look around. Can we save this conversation until tomorrow and enjoy the fact that we just won the actual championship?"

Coach's relentless urgency is what being hungry looks like.

Until 2019, we had never finished 1-2-3 in a race. That special year, we swept the top three spots four times. After one such weekend, I walked into our competition meeting expecting smiles and a bit of reveling in our achievement. We had won about half of the races to that point. But we were back to business. Nobody was laughing or high-fiving.

Don't get me wrong—we had done our celebrating at the track, and we were grateful for the great finish. But now we were back to work, and it was time to look at how to get better. Where did we make mistakes? How could we improve? I remember thinking, *Man, I can't imagine what this meeting would be like if we had stunk in the race.*

> **Successful teams and companies relentlessly pursue improvement.**

When Kyle won the championship race to end that 2019 season, we did a much better job of celebrating than in 2015. We enjoyed our accomplishment more. Monday morning was not miserable. I think the combination of finishing our greatest season ever on the first year since we lost J.D. gave us a greater sense of gratitude, and we appreciated just how difficult it was to do what we had just done.

We have the sense of urgency and hunger parts figured out at JGR. I hope we're seen as humble with our success, just like J.D. always was. But *gratefulness* is a theme that has become a priority as I lead our company. I want our employees to be grateful for their successes, and I realize that like everything else, that needs to be modeled at the top.

Gratefulness, humility, and hunger can coexist—and they should.

## TOPICS FOR REFLECTION

1. Trust and communication are important elements in any business relationship, but especially in an environment of urgency like ours at JGR. What are you doing to build trust with colleagues and supervisors in your organization? What does "managing up" look like in your role?

2. Coach's sense of urgency permeates our culture and is reflected in his saying that we need to stay humble but also stay hungry. What does "humble and hungry" look like in your organization? How about in your personal life? How do you fight against complacency in your successes?

PRINCIPLE 4

# PEOPLE ARE SOULS, NOT TRANSACTIONS

## TREAT PEOPLE AS SOULS, NOT TRANSACTIONS

# Chapter 13

# PEOPLE
# BEFORE PROFITS

PEOPLE ARE THE KEY TO FULFILLING a mission. More than that, each person is a unique soul, with hopes and dreams, valuable and wonderfully made—one in eight billion, in fact. From the start of JGR, Coach and J.D. demonstrated to me how to treat every person we interact with as a soul, not a transaction.

Treating people as transactions is viewing them as a means to an end, as a cog in the wheel to achieve our mission. Our mission matters, but people matter *more* than the mission. Treating our employees as souls means caring for them, valuing them not only for how they contribute to our mission but also for how they contribute to society.

People are wired to want to matter, especially at their jobs. When people matter, so do their dreams, their aspirations, and what makes them happy. Pastor Chip Ingram says every human wants to be able to answer three fundamental questions:

1. Who am I?
2. Where do I belong?
3. What am I supposed to do?

As leaders, we cannot answer those questions for everyone we interact with, but we can embrace and respect their journeys as they answer those questions for themselves. Every person we interact with every day—whether at our jobs, in our homes, or at the grocery store—has a soul and a purpose.

I watched J.D. model this day after day, year after year. Each interaction with J.D. made you feel like you were his best friend. Even back in college, he loved to invite people from outside our friend group to participate in our activities. He would talk to someone he thought needed a boost, and the next thing we knew, that person was part of our guys' weekend.

In a business world where people will shake your hand while looking over your shoulder for someone more important, J.D. always made the person whose hand he shook feel like they were the most important person to him.

Our biggest internal challenge as the company has grown from family to factory is competing at a world-class level while maintaining our three-part culture of honoring God, putting people before profits, and relentlessly pursuing winning.

J.D. often told me the responsibility he felt for our people was the one aspect of being company president that kept him awake at night. I used to tell Stacey, "Man, I'm glad I'm not J.D. I can't imagine the pressure of going to bed every night worried about so many families that depend on us." When I replaced J.D. as president, that worry transferred to me. I have so much respect now for how he handled our employees.

Caring about our people and our partners always will be a benchmark of Joe Gibbs Racing, because we try to prioritize people over profits.

With as many employees as we have now, the personal issues are nonstop. Financial problems. A young child with an illness. An older child gone wayward. A spouse who moved out of the house. A family member diagnosed as terminally ill.

We have had an in-house chaplain, Bob Dyar, from our start. For almost three decades, we have held a weekly chapel with a guest speaker and free lunch. On any given day, small-group Bible studies take place in conference rooms and break rooms within our facility.

On a personal level, Bob and his staff are available to employees to talk about grief, marriage, or life in general. I have felt Bob's impact. When my dad died, Bob prayed with my family, coached me through preparing my dad's eulogy, and drove with me to the funeral.

From a company standpoint, we schedule family events where our employees can bring their spouses and children. We have a family day when our employees and their families go to an amusement park, and we all make T-shirts. When the kids wear those T-shirts afterward, I hope they remember that day when we told their mom or dad, "Bring your families to the amusement park, and let's all have fun together."

Seeing our employees with their families reminds us of each person's value. They work hard here, and they put in long hours. Some of our positions require extensive travel and time away from home—the NASCAR schedule is thirty-six weekend races, with only two weekends off.

Our families sacrifice because of the careers we've chosen, and it is important to hold events where families are included so our company doesn't represent to them only a paycheck and the reason their spouse or parent is away from home so much. Each employee has loved ones counting on them. And they all are counting on us. How can we, as a company, talk about being a family at work without first caring about our employees' families at home?

Many companies are getting rid of their Christmas parties, largely for budget reasons. As long as Coach is around, we will have a Christmas party. The Christmas party is Joe's way of thanking our employees and their significant others, recognizing employees with awards, and enjoying being together. The party also is symbolic of our family, because families eat and celebrate together during holidays. The money we could save by canceling the party would not be worth the cost of telling our folks they are no longer worth a party.

We send birthday cards to employees' family members. We hold a company 5K every quarter that awards employees points toward their health insurance. We purchase season tickets to local sports teams and give our employees those tickets for free. If an employee doesn't join us at the amusement park, run the 5K, or use our free tickets, we still want them to know that our company offers those opportunities because we care.

One day Coy brought in food trucks unannounced and offered free lunches to all employees. About a hundred employees sought me out to express their appreciation for the lunch. I told Coy, "That's the best five grand we've ever spent."

In an era in which companies struggle to provide good benefits because of rising health care costs and other factors, we have committed to providing employees the best benefits package we can. When a representative of the company that handles our benefits came recently to meet with employees, she said, "We've been doing this for twenty years, and there's no company that has a benefits package like this. We advised your employer that they were doing too much compared to other companies, and they told us, 'Tough.'" I loved hearing that, not because we want to boast, but because it helps to have a third party tell our employees that we care enough to take extra steps on their behalf.

> Placing more value on people than the mission results in the people placing more value on the mission.

Communicating that our people matter was much easier when we felt like a family, so now we have to be more intentional about trying to communicate that on macro and micro levels. Like in any relationship, the little things demonstrate to our employees that they matter.

We've been fortunate to have employees with long tenures, and employee loyalty helps our on-track performance. I believe Todd came up with the brilliant idea of presenting a Rolex watch to employees on their tenth anniversary with JGR. (Granted, we were partly motivated by the fact that Todd, J.D., and I were coming up on *our* ten-year anniversaries.) But at that time, spending ten years with one team in NASCAR was unusual. Within a few years, we were handing out twenty-five to thirty watches each year. Then we had to start thinking about twenty-year gifts because so many people were staying with us. We decided to award an extra week of vacation. We still award watches at the ten-year mark, and we're giving away one to two dozen per year. Now at our company, an employee who has been here ten years might be on page four of our employee seniority list.

Admittedly, caring about employees is self-serving. The best way to go fast is to treat our people well, because motivated people perform better than disenchanted, disinterested people. To go fast, we need our people to care about our company. In order for our people to care about our company, the company needs to care about them. More specifically, we cannot only say we care—we must treat our people as souls and not transactions.

**Care Most for What Matters Most**
"Once you come to work for me," Coach says all the time, "I want you to retire here." And he means it. But more than that, when you work for Joe, you become part of the family.

One man served as Tony Stewart's spotter. He traveled to every race, and his wife stayed home to care for their two kids each weekend. She suffered an injury diving into a lake and was left paralyzed. Coach took time to visit her in the hospital and made a routine of calling to check on her.

While she was in rehab and as she and her husband tried to process how their new normal would look, we felt like one of the best ways to support them would be providing the family with a wheelchair-accessible van. We took up a collection on the shop floor. Tony contributed a significant amount, and Coach and J.D. offered to cover the rest. Within a few weeks, we had raised enough money as a JGR family to purchase a van for the family.

Chris works in our front office. Several years ago, his wife came down with a mysterious illness, and doctors in Charlotte could not arrive at a diagnosis. We prayed for Chris's wife in one of our Monday sessions, and Coach asked what was wrong. By that afternoon, Coach had called the Mayo Clinic himself and arranged for an appointment for Chris's wife that week. Coach offered Chris a team plane to fly to Minnesota for the appointment. Chris declined, but Coach insisted, and Chris and his wife were able to fly to Mayo Clinic and back the same day to be with their kids at home that night. Chris's wife continues to recover from her illness, and every Monday morning, Coach prays for her in our weekly meeting.

Coach has helped countless other employees when they or family members have suffered serious illness. That's what a family business does when it views its people as more than transactions.

We aim to hire good people, treat them well, and motivate them to buy in to treating our company like it's theirs. I say that not only as the president of Joe Gibbs Racing, tasked with maintaining a people-first culture. I also have been a recipient of the Gibbs family's care, going back to when I was growing up as a friend of J.D.'s.

When I was invited to attend a Redskins game, it was easy for me to think, *I'm going to tag along, but I don't deserve to be here.* Coach wouldn't allow me to feel that way. He made me feel not only as though I deserved to be there but also that I held a place of honor.

For all the good that Coach's kindness did for me as a teenager, I am more appreciative of how Coach honored me as an adult in front of my dad.

When I was in my late twenties, I brought my dad to a race. Coach learned that my dad was there, and he sought him out. Coach had only a couple of minutes to talk with him, but he gave my dad the time he could. Coach probably thought I was out of earshot, but I overheard Coach tell my dad, "The one thing about your son is, he is wise beyond his years. And I really value his wisdom."

I was a young guy who didn't know anything about anything, yet a Hall of Fame NFL coach was telling my dad that I was wise beyond my years. Coach doesn't say anything he does not mean. If Coach told my dad that, Coach believed it.

I think about that one sentence to this day because it changed me. Coach expressing his belief in me to my dad convinced me that I needed to trust my instincts more. I wasn't confident in conference room discussions and believed that the little I did speak was perhaps too much. From that point on, I felt open to participate more in those discussions because I knew Coach valued my wisdom.

> Even a small compliment, especially to someone less senior, can energize an employee for years.

But when I most felt Coach caring for me was when my dad became sick. Coach didn't know my dad well, but he asked for my dad's phone number and called him on a regular basis to ask how he was doing and to pray for him. He cared about my dad as a soul. When my dad passed away, Coach flew my family to the funeral and sat in the front row and nodded in approval as I eulogized Dad.

I know that I have a longer and closer relationship with Coach than any of our employees do, and he's not providing a plane to every employee who has a family member pass away. But I also know that Coach does more to show that he cares for his employees than anyone I know. And when I say *show*, I'm not talking about publicly showing so that others will notice; I'm talking about on an individual basis. He genuinely values people, and those most-often-unseen acts of kindness are far more significant than an owner of a company saying "Good job" to an employee.

I've mentioned the importance Coach places on people like our front desk receptionist and phone operator as front-line representatives of our company culture. He's great at relating with and motivating our drivers and sponsors. But he knows how to make people at every step on our organizational chart feel like they are great at performing their jobs—even if it's in a thirty-second chat. He calls people by name, asks how they're doing, and offers encouragement.

Coach cares. He views our company as a big family, and he is concerned about our employees' welfare, families, successes, and spiritual lives. Because he cares, he treats people as souls, not transactions. And he expects the same from leaders throughout our company.

From my experience, the stories that resonate most with Coach aren't the ones about winning a race or renewing a sponsor. He is moved far more when I tell him about talking with someone who attended one of Coach's ministry outreaches that impacted them to the point they had started attending church and their lives had changed. I remember when one of our employees was dealing with marital problems, he received counseling from our chaplain, and he and his wife reconciled and started attending church together. As I relayed that story to Coach, tears came to his eyes. Those are the moments Coach lives for, because despite all the accomplishments and public acknowledgments he has received in sports, people matter more to him than anything else.

## People over the Bottom Line

Even Coach would admit that it's easy with his personality type to get caught up in the minutiae of racing and to need a reset to what matters most. This is an area where we greatly miss J.D., and I'm trying to fill his role.

J.D. and his dad were an incredible duo. Coach is one of the most here-and-now people I've known. Forget projecting three years from now; he doesn't even like talking about next week! I'm always thinking about the future. Sometimes even the far future. A common exchange between Coach and me goes something like this:

Me: "If we do this now, we're going to be dealing with X, Y, and Z later."

Coach: "I don't care. We'll deal with it then."

Me: "Well, I'm going to prevent you from having to deal with it then, because I'm going to think about it now."

The way J.D. complemented his dad was by always focusing on how people were affected by our decisions and then choosing to do what was right. Coach is a fixer by nature. His goal is to cross off a task and move on to the next one—that thing about needing a battle to fight. Coach is not the technician here. That's why his obsession is to keep us funded and going fast. To Coach there is never enough sponsorship, we need to surround everyone with the best managers, and we need to align drivers with the best technical person, competition guy, and pit crew for them. If we don't, in his eyes, we are not providing everyone the tools they need to win races. If we win half the races, there were more we could have won. It's go, go, go with Coach. Keep pushing. But J.D. would come alongside his dad in discussions to talk about how people would be affected by decisions. To J.D., the fact that we *could* do something didn't mean that we *should*.

On account of how much J.D. cared for our employees, he would opt for doing what was right even if it didn't make business sense. He cared more about people than the bottom line. When sponsor-related issues came up that normally would lead to us pulling out the contract to see what we were required to do, J.D. would say, "Do what's right, not what's in the contract."

The funny thing is, from watching how J.D. ran our company, I noticed that the bottom line always seemed to turn out okay when J.D. prioritized taking care of people.

This might sound like a strange principle in a business book, but when we focus on our people and culture first, the numbers seem to work out fine. Here's why: employees who feel truly cared for by their leaders usually will give everything they have to their company out of loyalty. If they are first taken care of, they will be more passionate about the company, be willing to work extra hours, and give the best they have.

I practice the concept of deposits and withdrawals. Times come when we need to make withdrawals from our employees' personal accounts with us. It might be, "Hey, we're grinding; we're staying late to work on these cars. Sorry, but we're going to kill your Friday night." If we have made regular deposits beforehand—if we have shown we care about our employees by investing in them—they will be more willing to stay late on a Friday. But then we have to follow up by making more deposits to build up our account again. If we fail to do so, we will have a high turnover rate because we'll be churning through employees, and our performance will suffer.

Our mission is to go fast. Our objective is to win races. For us, winning is a by-product of treating our employees as valued souls. Believe me, if Coach can be obsessed with winning the way he is and still put his people first, just about anyone can.

Caring is not our reward to our employees for their performance. Performance is our employees' reward to us for caring about them.

## TOPICS FOR REFLECTION

1. Treating people as transactions means viewing them as a means to an end. Treating people as souls means valuing who they are as people. How would you rate yourself in this area? Think about your next few upcoming interactions. What specifically can you do to show you value the other person for who they are, rather than for what they contribute?

2. Coach's compliment about me to my dad filled my tank for years. Think about those around you—people above, equal to, and particularly anyone lower than you in the organizational structure. How can you be intentional in complimenting and encouraging them and in communicating to them how valuable they are?

## Chapter 14

# CONFLICT, HARD MESSAGES, AND CRISIS

As much as I lean on personality profiles in leadership, all personality types share one indisputable need: they must know how to deal with conflict to lead well.

Conflict never resolves itself. If ignored, conflict can cause irreparable damage to any relationship. Coach's proactive sense of urgency helps make him a master at conflict resolution. He refuses to allow conflict to fester.

Two of our drivers had a run-in during a race weekend. Back at the office, Coach brought the drivers together and made them sit across from each other to work through their issues. The following weekend happened to be one of the rare races when Coach was on a personal trip, and he was not planning to come to the track until Sunday, the day of the Cup race. During Saturday's practice session, the drivers had another run-in on the track. That carried over to the garage, where the two almost had to be separated.

When Coach heard of the flare-up, he didn't wait until the next day to address the situation—he immediately left his trip to come to the track. He arrived late Saturday night and demanded that both drivers meet him at eleven o'clock. He made them sit facing each other and allowed each to give his side of the story. Then Coach talked. It was a pretty long session, which concluded with the drivers shaking hands before walking out of the trailer. The next morning, race day, the two were able to focus on the race instead of each other.

Here are four crucial aspects of how Coach handled the situation:

» He dealt with it as soon as possible, even leaving a vacation to address the situation.

» Instead of solving the problem for the drivers, he forced them to resolve it between themselves.

» He brought the drivers face-to-face rather than making a three-way phone call or communicating by text. Conflict resolution is infinitely more effective face-to-face.

» He knew resolving conflict would better position each driver to succeed during the race.

That's one example. Coach has left vacations and has dropped his plans to fly out to meet with unhappy sponsors in order to respond urgently to conflict.

Handling confrontation seems to come easy for Coach, perhaps even energizing him. After all, his coaching career was one huge conflict played out on a field, and he thrived under that pressure. I, on the other hand, am nonconfrontational by nature and, since becoming president, have seen my role change to where I spend most of my day dealing with conflicts of some type. Conflict exhausts me.

I am uncomfortable in nonpeaceful environments. If a relationship is unsettled or a crisis is unsolved, I have difficulty falling asleep at night. If I can control the situation, I don't let the sun go down on conflict—especially when I am not involved in the conflict. One of my strong suits is inserting myself into conflict and, without taking a side, calming the two people who are angry with each other. The closer my relationship with the people involved, the more passionate I am about bringing a peaceful resolution.

> Leaders do not have to enjoy conflict,
> but they must be willing to deal with it swiftly.

Leadership is rolling up your sleeves and dealing directly with conflict.

A key element of my being a peacemaker is building trust with people during times of peace. That way, when conflict arises, I already have made deposits in their bank of trust and they will be more likely to understand my perspective. By making those deposits, I have earned their trust and can speak into the conflict.

A good peacemaker has the ability to step in between two people and help resolve their conflict in such a manner that one doesn't walk away as the winner and the other as the loser. Mediating a compromise helps, but the ultimate secret to a good negotiation is that both parties walk away feeling like they got a great deal.

Fun? Not usually. But necessary for the health of a company. And for a company that values relationships, it's necessary for the health of the individual relationships within the company.

### Blessed (and Exhausted) Is the Peacemaker

In the early days, we experienced a crisis about once a week. Now there are several each day. Most have a common element: people.

If you ask my wife my best personality trait, she will say I am a peacemaker. But one incident in particular required all the peacemaking mojo I could muster.

We had a partner who owned his own company. He had a reputation for being demanding, sometimes unreasonably so. He also had a volatile temper, which I'd had the good fortune of never seeing. For those who were on the man's good side, he also could be very generous.

The man visited our office one day, and while on the shop floor, he became frustrated about the positioning of his company's logo on a car. In front of a large number of our employees, he started loudly cursing. Then he took out his anger on one of our employees who services our sponsors, screaming at her and cussing her out. Another employee came to me later and told me the sponsor had created quite a scene and upset this particular employee.

I've always felt using profanity is uncalled for, especially in a business setting. I believe we should show our best at work. We don't wear our worst clothes to work, so why would we use our worst language? The sponsor's screaming at one of our employees didn't sit well with me.

Two options came to mind. First, I could do nothing because he was an important sponsor. Or, second, I could call him up and tell him he was an idiot and get into a big fight with him.

Both options had merit. Fortunately, I chose neither.

I knew he was angry with us, and as a peacemaker, I needed to resolve the matter. But I also needed to point out his behavior so it wouldn't occur again. I called him, and the minute he answered his phone, he started cursing at me. I had barely started what I wanted to say when he interrupted with "I don't want to hear it. Your people are incompetent."

I told the man that I wanted to meet with him, but he wasn't interested. His company was within driving distance of our office, so I drove to his building and showed up at his front desk unannounced.

I told the receptionist I was there to meet with him.

"Do you have an appointment?" she asked.

"No."

"Does he know you're coming?"

"No." I added, "And I doubt he wants to see me."

She called his office, hung up, and told me, "He's in a meeting."

I knew he was in the office.

"I'm okay to wait," I said. "Tell him I'll be here when he's finished with his meeting."

I took a seat, and two minutes later, the receptionist told me, "You can see him now."

When I entered his office, he appeared uncomfortable. Instead of looking me in the eye, he shuffled around in his chair.

But I didn't let him have it. Instead, I asked, "Can you walk me through what happened?"

He yelled at me for what felt like thirty minutes. I didn't raise my voice to him until he unleashed a string of profanities. After a two-hour meeting, he apologized, and he agreed to apologize to our employee by phone. Then we shook hands.

I had to tap into every bit of strength I could muster to not yell back or call him names. We'd had a good relationship to that point, and I wanted to work through this first problem so we could continue with a good working relationship. We *had* made a mistake with his logo, and I apologized and assured him we would correct our error. I showed empathy.

But I also stood up for our employee and expressed how unacceptable his behavior had been. I did so while still showing the man respect (even though I didn't feel like he deserved it at that point). I also let him know that based on what I knew from our relationship, he was better than his behavior on our shop floor and that I held him to a higher standard.

I tell that story because of the valuable lesson I learned that day while getting cussed out: a key tenet of being a peacemaker is to not make things personal—to attack the behavior, not the person.

And, yes, that meeting exhausted me!

## Delivering Hard Messages

Just as the amount of conflict to address increased when I became president, so did the number of hard messages I needed to deliver.

Few people enjoy delivering tough messages or bad news, whether daily inconvenient messages to coworkers or devastating life-and-death news. Regardless of the topic or level of difficulty, delivering tough messages is part of life and business. No matter what your job is or what stage of your career you're in, you will probably have to deliver some hard messages, whether it is talking to a boss about a raise, confronting a coworker about a frustration, giving an employee an unfavorable review, or telling a client you've screwed up.

A combination of four elements is essential when delivering a tough message, whether communicating to an employee, the entire company, a sponsor, or a customer: show empathy, be honest, offer solutions, and do what's right to stay on mission.

Entering these types of conversations requires asking several questions of yourself:

> » Empathy: *How will what I am about to share affect the person or group I'm sharing it with?*
> » Honesty: *How can I be as straightforward as possible with as much detail as I can provide?*
> » Solutions: *What is the next step or follow-up?*
> » Mission: *How will this situation affect the big picture of what we desire to accomplish?*

In our industry, delivering tough messages happens a lot. As JGR leadership's resident feeler, few topics affect me more than moving on from a driver. When Carl Edwards unexpectedly retired, we promoted Daniel Suárez to fill Carl's seat. Two years later, we had to deliver the excruciating news to Danny that we no longer had a spot for him in our car.

Danny was an international success story. From modest means in Mexico, he moved to the United States by himself, learned English, and worked his way up to eventually win the 2016 Xfinity Series with us as the first foreign-born champion in a national NASCAR series. More important, Danny was a good person—funny, charming, a hard worker, and a student of the sport. He was everything a team looks for in a driver and a teammate.

Circumstances and timing can make or break careers in sports, especially in NASCAR. When we brought Danny up to our Cup team, the timing was perfect with Carl's departure, Danny's Xfinity championship, and a sponsor being tied to Danny. Two years later, circumstances and timing worked against Danny.

In any given fall, we contemplate dozens of scenarios that could play out for the upcoming season. No matter how many scenarios we imagined, none could have accounted for what occurred in the fall of 2018. Much like with Carl following the 2016 season, one phone call sent us scrambling.

Furniture Row Racing, a team for which we had supplied technical support as part of an alliance, decided to shut down. The circumstances behind their decision were detailed and difficult. Considering FRR's Cup championship with Martin Truex Jr. in 2017, the team's departure from the sport was not among our planned-for possibilities.

FRR was part of the Toyota team, and Toyota loved Martin. He had won that championship, and his sponsors, Bass Pro Shops and Auto-Owners Insurance, had committed to staying with him wherever he ended up the next season. Johnny Morris, Bass Pro's CEO, is one of the nicest, most well-respected sponsors in the garage.

We knew we had to act fast because there would be a feeding frenzy of teams wanting to lure a champion driver with top-tier sponsorship in tow. If we didn't sign Martin, he would go to a Ford or Chevy team, which would be a big loss for Toyota, our biggest partner. With Martin's talent, he would make our team better. Additionally, if he went elsewhere, we would have to compete against him for years to come. I have always said that losing a driver to another team is twice as damaging as losing a driver to retirement, because you lose his speed while making a competitor faster.

Our other three drivers were under contract for the following year and tied to sponsorship arrangements. Danny's contract was set to expire at year's end, although we had every expectation of extending his deal and bringing him back.

Our two options were to keep Danny and let Martin go to another team, or to sign Martin and let Danny move on. The questions we had to ask ourselves were, What is the best decision for all our employees? What decision best adds to our mission of going fast? How do we make that decision while treating each person and company involved as a soul and not a transaction?

We signed Martin, not because Danny had done anything wrong and not because of a strict plan we had to stick with. We were a performance-based sports team bent on going fast and had a rare chance to add a Hall of Fame–caliber athlete to our team. An NFL team not looking for a quarterback might change its mind when Tom Brady becomes available, and we were our sport's equivalent of that team.

But the soul/transaction part meant that although signing Martin was the right decision for Joe Gibbs Racing, our choice affected many people—and they weren't just cogs in our machine; they were souls whom we cared about.

We had to sit down with Danny's sponsors and explain our situation. They were gracious yet disappointed. Because we were honest and empathetic and explained how our decision fit our mission, the sponsors understood. Most agreed to move on with Danny.

We met with Danny for what was a very difficult conversation. We were as honest as we could be about our decision. We knew this would cause a huge setback for his career, but we had an unusual opportunity, and we owed it to our people to make ourselves better. We talked about helping Danny land with another team, which we did, and worked with his sponsors to do the same. I still keep up with Danny and root for him. He's a good man, and I hope he would call me a friend.

Coach could have viewed talking to Danny as a box to check off. But Danny is a soul and a friend, and we wanted to do everything we could for him and his career, even though it wouldn't be with us. That conversation was really hard. Many conversations are in business and in life. I still get sick to my stomach thinking about the dozens of conversations like that we've had over the years. They don't seem to get any easier for me.

Experience has taught me that people on the receiving end of difficult messages do not want a flowery speech or beating around the bush. Being forthright but compassionate with a tough message provides a clear definition of the news. As with casting vision, clear communication is essential in delivering bad news, because bad news presents enough problems on its own.

## Running into Crisis

When it comes to crisis, I love employees who are like the real-life Desmond Doss portrayed in the movie *Hacksaw Ridge*.

Desmond Doss served as an army medic in World War II. Doss, a conscientious objector on religious grounds, refused to carry a rifle. At the battle of Okinawa, Doss's battalion was ordered to retreat from fighting at a site known as Hacksaw Ridge. Doss refused to leave and made trip after trip—alone—into the kill zone to retrieve wounded soldiers. He carried the soldiers to the edge of a cliff and lowered them to safety, returning back into the kill zone, each time praying, "Lord, please help me get one more." Doss is estimated to have rescued seventy-five soldiers, a feat that earned him the Medal of Honor.

NASCAR is nothing like war, but I love that image of running into battle. I want employees who will run *into* a crisis instead of turning away.

I sometimes think my job title should be "crisis negotiator." When approached with the line "We need to discuss this crisis," my response often is "Which one are we talking about?" Take your pick of topics— a driver did something that bothered a sponsor, an employee is frustrated with a coworker, a sponsor agreement is up for renewal and needs extra TLC to get the deal done, NASCAR is contemplating a rules change that will adversely affect our performance. The list goes on and on.

One example of a driver-sponsor crisis occurred in November 2011. It was Friday of the race weekend at Texas Motor Speedway, and I had planned to leave Charlotte on Sunday morning for the Cup race. Kyle Busch was racing in the trucks series race Friday night, as he often does. Kyle became frustrated with another driver, and during caution laps, he intentionally wrecked the driver. It was late at night, and as I watched the event unfold on TV, I asked myself, *Did that really just happen?* I knew this was about to become a major crisis.

Sure enough, the phone started ringing, and the next morning I was on the first flight to Dallas. NASCAR suspended Kyle for that weekend's Cup race. Mars, the primary sponsor of Kyle's Cup car, was rightfully unhappy.

Chris Helein, our communications lead, is the guy to call first when there is a crisis because he stays cool and thinks straight. I asked Chris to fly to Dallas so we could hunker down, develop a plan, and start calling people. Our weekend was not going to be fun.

Among those joining us to develop a strategy for the battle ahead was a group of people who were not required to be there. All had other things they could be doing, but they came to our meeting because they knew the issue was important to me and the company, and they wanted to offer options for our plan. They came because they cared about how we handled the matter. They ran into the crisis.

Those are the kinds of employees I want on my team. People who are bought in to a culture and sold on the mission will want to run into crisis for the sake of the team.

> People who are bought in to a culture and its mission will want to run into crisis for the sake of the team.

Too many people avoid crises. The minute a tough decision needs to be made, or the need for an uncomfortable phone call or in-person meeting arises, they disappear. Because conflict never resolves itself, those who flee are assuming someone else will clean up the mess. Someone's natural bent might not be crisis negotiator—trust me, mine isn't—but it is a skill that everyone should develop to create the most value for their company.

Most leaders reading this book could likely pause here and write a list of names of their employees who will run into a crisis and those who will run away. Which kind are you?

## Battling the Conflict Within

There is a type of conflict that isn't talked about enough in business leadership books: internal conflict. Conflicts that we've dealt with or are dealing with in our individual lives—such as mental illness, physical challenges, or perhaps family crises—affect how we handle all other types of conflict.

I certainly have had my share of all of those. But my biggest internal conflict has been my twitches—more specifically, my diagnosis in elementary school of Tourette's syndrome (TS), something I have not spent enough time talking about in my life. I've met with parents of kids with TS, and more often than not, the parents have started crying when I share my experience with TS and describe how I have dealt with it.

I recently had an extended conversation with my friend Marty Smith, an ESPN reporter who has covered NASCAR, among other sports, for many years. Marty's son has TS, and from talking with Marty, his son's case sounded similar to mine. As I talked about my TS, I felt Marty's emotion as he listened to someone who was able to articulate what his son was going through and feeling. I then used my example to encourage Marty that his son will be able to adapt to TS and turn out fine.

Even though I had talked with numerous parents before my conversation with Marty, our discussion opened my eyes as I remembered how I had been unable to articulate to my parents what I was going through and feeling and how it was so difficult for them to understand what it meant for me to have TS.

A survey conducted by the Tourette Association of America in 2018 found that 51 percent of adults and 32 percent of parents of children with TS have either contemplated suicide or participated in self-harming behaviors.[3] That is a scary stat but one that, having suffered with TS for so long, does not surprise me.

Tourette's, as it is often called, is a disorder of the nervous system that causes people to experience tics or sudden and repeated twitches, movements, or sounds. The tics are motor (body movements) or vocal (sounds). Common examples are blinking, shoulder shrugs, blurting out a word or phrase, and humming.

My symptoms started in fifth grade with uncontrollable chewing of my lip. That led to facial twitches. Then it was consecutive deep breaths, or mimicking a sound or movement over and over, to the point of exhaustion. I lay awake at night trying to figure out what was wrong with me. My parents were going through a divorce at the time, and they sent me to a child psychologist, who believed my tics were an emotional response to the trauma of the divorce. I met with the psychologist for the next two years, but my symptoms remained. Finally, a series of frightening tests revealed that I had Tourette's.

My symptoms worsened in high school, and I was prescribed Haldol. The medicine wiped me out physically, and some of my teachers called my parents to express their concerns that I didn't seem like myself. Because the side effects were as bad as or worse than the Tourette's, I was taken off the medication. I've remained medically untreated since.

Because of media portrayals, Tourette's often is associated with people who blurt out profanities. Coprolalia is the medical word for that condition, which occurs in only 10 percent of people with TS.[4] I did not have coprolalia, but I did experience some strange manifestations. One was the urge to feel the sensation of twirling. I would walk down a hallway at school and start twirling like a bad ballerina. Another was kicking my own rear end. That's not easy to do, but when I didn't want to, I could!

Playing baseball, I would sometimes walk to home plate kicking my own rear end. That earned me the nickname "Rooster." You can imagine how well both of those gems went over in high school.

I already was a late bloomer physically and the smallest kid in my high school. Add in the worsening tics at an age when even a "normal" teenage boy is likely to deal with identity and self-worth issues, and let's just say it was hard not to struggle with self-confidence.

I compensated by developing a good sense of humor. It must have worked, because although I endured teasing, I did not experience the level of bullying that would be expected. I did get stuffed in a trash can my first week of school—straight out of a movie, I know—but, overall, it wasn't too bad.

At night I struggled to fall asleep because of the constant twitching, and even though I did not have a relationship with God at the time, I would stare at the ceiling above my bed and plead with him to take my horrible symptoms away from me.

Studying was as difficult as sleeping, because my symptoms were at their worst when I was in a quiet setting. Tourette's kept me from sitting still, and I would twitch or grind my teeth or chew my lip. All I could do to help was turn on music or the TV to disrupt the silence, which was not conducive for focusing on my homework or falling asleep.

I couldn't articulate to my parents what I was experiencing, and I felt alone. Like no one understood—because I didn't know anyone who could understand.

Unable to prevent myself from chewing the inside of my mouth, one of my go-to twitches, I developed a nasty gash on the inside of my cheek. My parents took me to an oral surgeon, who fit me with a mouth device to protect my cheek.

"You've got to stop chewing on yourself for two days, or this device isn't going to work," the oral surgeon told me.

"The reason I'm here," I told him, "is because I can't stop chewing on it."

I turned to my mom and asked her, "Can you explain to him that I have a disease and that I can't stop?"

She couldn't.

"There's no medical condition that makes you chew on your lip," the doctor said. "You just need to stop."

*Thanks for the great advice!* (Eye roll.)

The absolute worst thing for someone with Tourette's is for the Tourette's to be noticed. Someone with TS can be at lunch with a group and a tic occurs. If anyone in the group makes a noticeable facial reaction or asks, "Why are you twitching?" that causes the person with TS to feel a wave of pressure to *not* tic and, instead, makes them more susceptible to continued tics. If no one at the table reacts to a tic, that removes the pressure and helps suppress further urges. I know that sounds bizarre, but that is what it's like with Tourette's.

When Stacey and I started dating in college, you can imagine my fear that the twitches would bother her. She was the first person who truly made me feel they were a nonfactor. Early in our relationship, we talked about my Tourette's, and she said, "I honestly don't even notice. It's just part of you." Her comfort with my Tourette's and the fact that it didn't matter to her made it matter less to me. I didn't think about my Tourette's when I was with Stacey.

Fortunately, TS symptoms often lessen into adulthood, and that has been true in my case. I still exhibit symptoms, but mostly internal ones that aren't noticeable to most people. Tourette's usually comes with some OCD and anxiety traits, both of which I also deal with.

Dealing with TS nonstop through my formative years made me mentally tough. My condition played a big role in making me who I am as a man and, now, a company president. I realize that every interaction with someone I have is not just a transaction; it is an interaction with a soul—a living person who is dealing with something, whether it's a disability, a mental illness, or another internal struggle like I have experienced. How I choose to help that person deal with or feel about whatever thorn they have is part of my mission every day.

How we deal with internal conflict shapes how we deal with the many external conflicts we face in life.

## TOPICS FOR REFLECTION

1. Conflict, hard conversations, and crises are things that every person will have to deal with at some point, and for leaders, developing the skills to handle these well is crucial. How would you rate yourself at handling conflict at work? How about in your other spheres of influence? Would your coworkers or boss say you are someone who runs into a crisis or runs away from one?

2. The internal conflicts we inevitably face determine how we handle external conflicts. What internal conflicts have shaped you? How can you use what you have learned (and are learning) from those conflicts to equip you to better empathize with others dealing with conflicts in their own lives?

# Chapter 15

# BUSINESS IS RELATIONSHIPS

As I explain when I speak to university business schools, the most important elements of a healthy business relationship are communication, trust, mutual understanding, and respect. Those are the same elements that make up a healthy friendship and even a healthy marriage.

Business is like any other relationship, and for almost three decades now, I have heard Coach preach that business is simply building relationships. More important, I have watched Coach live out that idea by intentionally keeping relationships the focus of business. As with a marriage, business relationships need to be intentional and sometimes require simply showing up.

At JGR, we go to great lengths and sometimes inconveniences to meet face-to-face with people.

In 2014, we were contacted by Carlos Slim Domit, a Mexican businessman and a big fan of motorsports. Carlos's father, Carlos Slim Helú, is a business mogul who at various times has been named by business magazines as the richest man in the world. When Carlos called, he shared his dream of seeing Mexico's best drivers ascend to the top levels of motorsports around the world. Carlos had already entered into Formula 1 racing and wanted to expand into NASCAR. Mexican-born Daniel Suárez drove for Carlos's group.

Diversity had long been a passion of J.D.'s. A decade earlier, we had started a diversity program with the help of NFL legend Reggie White. J.D. was intentional about recruiting young, diverse drivers. In the Cup Series, Daniel; Bubba Wallace, currently NASCAR's only African American driver; and Aric Almirola, of Cuban descent, all came through JGR's diversity program.

Carlos sent a team of his associates to meet with us, and we wound up forming not only a partnership but also a friendship with Carlos. Danny was twenty-two and appeared ready to compete in NASCAR, so we signed Danny to race in the Xfinity Series. Carlos offered his connections to help us acquire sponsorships tied to Danny.

Our relationship with Carlos exemplifies how Coach values personal relationships in business. Whenever we needed to have an important conversation with Carlos—updates on sponsors or our development plans for Danny—Coach would say, "Let's go see him." Sometimes Coach would say that even when we didn't need to have an important conversation. At times, he just wanted to meet with Carlos in person. Carlos was based in Mexico City. I would ask Coach if a teleconference would work instead, and based on what I knew of Carlos, I was sure he would be fine with us calling him. But Coach would insist that we fly down to Mexico for our meeting, and then we would turn right around and fly back. We made at least half a dozen of those trips.

After Danny won the Xfinity championship, we wanted to present Carlos with a piece of artwork. Boris, our in-house digital guru and a talented artist, painted a portrait of Danny. Instead of sending the painting to Carlos, Coach delivered the artwork in person to express his gratitude for introducing us to Danny.

I still believe that Carlos would have been okay with teleconferences, but I also saw firsthand how he responded to our coming to meet with him in person. Carlos was one of the most influential men in the world, and when we said we wanted to come visit, he opened his schedule to make room for us. By meeting face-to-face and—as Coach would emphasize—on Carlos's turf, trust was quickly built between Carlos and us. I believe that trust would have developed over time through teleconferences and occasional in-person meetings, but Coach is intentional about building relationships. Ours with Carlos grew quicker through our meetings than it would have otherwise.

On another occasion, when Monster Energy was one of our sponsors, I updated Coach one morning on an issue that had come up involving a driver and the direction of our future with Monster. As I was going over what Coach should share with Monster in a phone call, he said, "We ought to go see them. We need to talk about this over dinner."

Thirty minutes later, Coach's assistant called to inform me the plane would leave in an hour.

"For where?" I asked.

"California," he replied. "You're going to have dinner with the owner of Monster."

"Today?" I asked.

"Yes."

An hour later, we took off on a cross-country flight, had a two-hour dinner and discussion with Monster's owner, and flew home that night. (This also speaks to the sense of urgency with which Coach operates.)

Because Coach valued our relationship with Monster, the face-to-face time with Monster's owner was worth the effort. Coach doesn't always choose what is most convenient or most efficient, but he does choose what is most beneficial to a relationship—business or personal. And that usually means being present.

## A Model in Being Strategic

Part of my belief in treating business as relationships has been impacted by a personal relationship. Rick Beckwith has been my mentor for more than thirty years. He was the Young Life ministry leader I met at J.D.'s house in high school, and we still talk most Wednesday mornings on my way to work. Every day in the office, I try to put into practice lessons I have learned from Rick.

From the class of 1987 that I graduated high school with, I still have a group of about a dozen guys I am close with. We have a group text called "Band of Brothers," and we have actually grown tighter since high school. In fact, there are some members of the group I wasn't especially close to in school. In many ways, Rick is responsible for the special bond our group enjoys. After we went our separate ways for college, Rick hosted summer get-togethers with Bible studies designed to get us back together and to keep our relationships going.

Rick is the most intentional person I've met, and he has modeled for me how to be strategic with people.

Back in high school, because Rick always had his Day-Timer with him, we joked that he should be a national spokesman for the company. He held his Day-Timer open as he talked, and at the conclusion of a conversation, he would write a note to follow up with that person and say something like "I'm going to check back with you in two weeks on what we just prayed about." And he would. Every time. Sometimes, his follow-up would be to ask a very pointed question about an area that person had been struggling in. For two weeks, we knew Rick's question was coming, and that served as needed accountability for us.

Rick was not afraid to ask the questions that no one else in our lives would ask, because Rick was eternity-focused. Rick must have strategized about our conversations beforehand, because when he was with us, he found a way to maximize every minute he spent with each of us. There was no idle hangout time with Rick. Everything was purposeful. You could say he was good about staying on his mission as a spiritual leader.

The characteristic of Rick that most impacted me as a teenager skeptical of religion was that he cared for me. I spent a year and a half watching J.D. live out his faith while at the same time telling Rick I thought Christians were brainwashed. Although I had not responded favorably to what Rick considered the most important thing, he never stopped wanting to spend time with me. After many of our weekly meetings, our group would pack out a McDonald's, and it seemed like every time, Rick found a way to sit at my table. He would offer to meet one-on-one, and I would do it because I never felt like Rick was judging me or giving me some kind of ultimatum before giving up on me.

Rick gave me opportunities to ask any questions I wanted, and I posed some hard questions to him, as well as some obnoxious questions like "If God can do anything, can he make a rock so big that even he can't move it?" No matter how much I tried to send a signal that I didn't care about faith or the message Rick was sharing, I never felt like he did not care for me as a person.

This might sound odd, but Rick didn't stop caring for me *after* I became a Christian either. What I mean is that I wasn't a "believer" box that he needed to check so he could move on to the next person on his list. I am more years removed from high school than I prefer to admit, but there is a reason I am still calling my high school Young Life leader on the way to the office on a regular basis.

Rick has grown to love racing, and I know that after every race our team wins, one of my first congratulatory texts will be from him.

Rick still takes part in my group of buddies' summer get-togethers. He shows up with a printed itinerary. Devotions and meals are scheduled, and he brings questions and topics that we all discuss to share our thoughts with each other. (Rick obviously is not a feeler on Myers-Briggs; he's a thinker.) We leave each time with a takeaway that will help us continue to grow as husbands, dads, and believers.

The impact Rick has made on my life is difficult to put into words. Then I think about the fact that our relationship has grown for more than three decades. Rick is ten years older than me, and I wonder how many other people like me he mentors. Talk about leaving a legacy!

Rick serves as a great model of leadership for me. I regularly ask myself questions based on what I have learned from Rick:

» How can I be intentional with every interaction?
» How can I encourage, challenge, and hold others accountable?
» What am I doing to help folks who work with me be better, whether they are above, equal to, or below me?
» Are there a few folks in my life whom I am intentionally pouring into in a mentoring relationship? (Rick had many more than a few.)

As a type-A, efficient person who sets a schedule and tries to stick to it, when I am at a race and need to walk through the garage, I have held my phone up to my ear pretending to be on a call. Then I give a head nod or quick wave as I pass through to avoid being stopped for a conversation. As you can see, I'm a work in progress.

I have tried during my career to be intentional about asking what's going on in people's lives. I want to ask about their families. For some reason in a work environment, people tend to not open up about their lives or their families. I recognize the need to ask for information that often goes unsaid without prompting. When people ask about my wife or kids, their interest makes me feel good. I love talking about my wife and kids. I want to provide others that same opportunity.

I also have tried to become a better listener with my employees and follow up with questions like "How can we be better?" or "How can I help you?"

From Rick, I have learned that treating people as souls and not transactions affects the questions we ask. If someone is considered a transaction, the questions focus on performance. If someone is treated as a soul, the questions focus on personal growth.

> **Transaction-based conversations center on performance; soul-based conversations center on people.**

Our level of care for people is revealed through our conversations—both the questions we ask and how well we listen.

### Awe in the Family

As much as Rick, Coach, and J.D. have taught me the principle of treating people as souls and not transactions, I also need to talk about the impact three other people have made on me—my sons. Being a dad has been the greatest joy of my life. I have worried so much about imparting wisdom to my sons, but the truth is they have ended up teaching me even more than I have taught them.

Evan and Austin are often identified as one: "the Alpern twins." They do share many of the same traits, but each, along with their little brother, Collin, has so many unique qualities I admire.

Austin is a born leader. He has always been wise beyond his years, and he is levelheaded in any situation. I often call or text him in stressful circumstances to ask for his wisdom. He is such a gifted communicator. He's the friend who isn't afraid to run into a crisis. He is disciplined and ambitious. After he graduated from college, he decided to run a trail half-marathon in the woods. He trained for only two weeks and finished fifth overall. Then he ran a full marathon two weeks later—just because. He sees the world as black and white and, with deep compassion, struggles with injustices. (I thought he should become a judge.) He spent part of two summers at a special-needs orphanage in China.

Austin has world-class organizational skills that, despite his crazy schedule, enabled him to edit much of this book in his spare moments. In a competitive, me-first world, Austin values people, which, like Rick, he demonstrates by how he treats them.

Evan's number one CliftonStrengths trait is woo (winning over others). Evan possesses an off-the-charts EQ. He is a great empathizer who can articulate feelings. That's a powerful combination. Evan demonstrates to me how to lead from the heart. He is passionate about work that is meaningful. He founded a club in college to teach technology to students with disabilities, and he has passionately supported Joy Prom, a prom for teenagers and adults with cognitive and physical disabilities. He also led philanthropy at his fraternity.

Evan sees the world years from now—he is a big-picture guy who can also handle details. His sweet spot is in front of people because of the value he places on anyone he is face-to-face with. Highly self-aware, he is as comfortable one-on-one as he is in front of five thousand, as he was when he delivered the keynote speech at his high school graduation without a single note card. I relate to Evan's "feeler" trait and have watched him become a high achiever while wrestling with the difficulties of the world with compassion and empathy.

Collin is extrovert number five in our family, although almost an introvert compared to the rest of us. If ever there was a complement to a family, it's Collin. He is a consummate peacemaker with the ability to diffuse any tension. He is a peaceful voice of reason. He holds firm, strong convictions but demonstrates them with meekness and winsomeness. He is in the 1 percent of the population that is ambidextrous, which is appropriate, because that's how I describe him relationally given his ability to blend with any group. Collin is less about the *do* and more about the *who*. He is a unique thinker who often takes a different angle. He loves well and is loyal.

My boys are fountains to so many, because they deliver more than they are paid—well, Collin doesn't get paid anything yet, but he will!—and they treat people like souls, not transactions. Clearly they take after their mother!

People ask if my sons will someday work for me, and I answer that they need to change the world first. Maybe they will hire me someday, and I can be an intern for them!

## President Bush, Kid Rock, and Jesus

Because business is relationships, developing relationships is what I love most about my job. In the process, I meet interesting people. Whether it was hosting LeBron James and his family at Bristol with Coca-Cola/Powerade (and not taking a single photo with him because it was in the days before all phones had cameras) or Tom Cruise at a race in Richmond, getting to meet folks is a huge perk.

No race provides more opportunities to meet interesting people than the Daytona 500. Daytona is my favorite race for several reasons. Because the race starts a new season, it represents a fresh beginning filled with hope for the year ahead. Also, every year for the past two and a half decades, our family has traveled to Daytona earlier than for other races and stayed at the same beach house. Each year, my wife, Stacey, has snapped a photo of me with my three sons on the back porch. Among my most-prized possessions are all the photos displayed to show how the boys (and I) have aged. We have twenty-four years of iterations of the picture.

More celebrities attend the Daytona 500 than any other race, and the 2004 race was a special one for Norm Miller and Interstate Batteries. Mel Gibson's film *The Passion of the Christ* was scheduled to be released later that month, and for the number 18 car at the biggest race of the year, Norm chose to convert the traditional green Interstate Batteries paint scheme into a movie billboard with the film's logo on the hood.

The day before the race, I learned that our team would host Jim Caviezel, the actor who played Jesus in the film. Jim and his wife, Kerri, would arrive the morning of the race, and Stacey and I would take care of them for the day. I was pretty excited to be in charge of "Jesus" for his first race visit.

President George W. Bush—this was before we became best friends at the White House—was on hand as the race's Grand Marshal. Because of security for the president, the Secret Service had the entire pit area on lockdown for three hours before the start of the race. No one was allowed in or out of the pits. Anyone in the pits when the shutdown began was stuck inside an area a few hundred yards in length. That happened to us, and there was no going to get anything to eat or drink, which made it a challenge to host a Hollywood star who had arrived on a red-eye.

Jim and Kerri were tired and hungry. Jim is a Christian, and his denominational beliefs included him taking Communion on Sunday mornings, regardless of location or Secret Service lockdown. Jim politely informed me of his beliefs and asked if I could help facilitate Communion consisting of real wine and bread given and blessed by a priest.

Here's the scene: the actor who would soon become known for playing the most iconic representation of Jesus Christ in film history had just asked me to find wine, bread, and a priest inside a NASCAR pit area locked down by the Secret Service.

A strategic problem-solver by personality and trade, my brain shifted into go mode. I reached out to our chaplain, Bob, and asked if he knew of a priest at the race. He did, and he offered to contact the priest for me. I knew that Richard Childress, one of the team owners, owned a vineyard. I sent someone to Richard's motor coach to ask if he had a bottle of wine he could donate. He did.

Finding a piece of bread was easy, and thanks to our chaplain, who discovered a quiet location at the media center, the priest conducted a private chapel for Jim and Kerri at Daytona International Speedway.

JGR has a race-day tradition of gathering in Joe's motor coach to pray. Jim, Kerri, and Norm joined us. In what would become my most memorable pre-race prayer, we gathered in a circle with Stacey, Coach, J.D., Norm Miller, and me holding hands and praying with "Jesus" for the Daytona 500. We also prayed that God would place his favor on the movie project. Adding to the already surreal scene, as Jim prayed, a gust of wind rattled the motor coach.

One of the greatest images of Southern culture is the singing of "The Star-Spangled Banner" at a NASCAR race. That day, because President Bush knew Coach and the president of Home Depot, the president stood by us during the national anthem. Nearby sat a large vehicle with the back doors swung open and a guy manning a revolving machine gun that made him look like the gunner in the back of a fighter plane. Secret Service agents were all around, armed with semiautomatic weapons.

Tony Stewart's pit guest for the race was Kid Rock. As LeAnn Rimes sang the anthem, I looked around to notice that I was standing by Coach, President Bush, Kid Rock, and the actor who played Jesus. Only at a NASCAR race. What a great sport and country!

## TOPICS FOR REFLECTION

1. Business is relationships, and relationships require intentionality and care to grow. Make a list of relationships inside and outside of your organization that you can be more intentional with in the coming weeks, which may benefit from you just showing up.

2. Transaction-based conversations center on performance; soul-based conversations center on people. Be deliberate this week with making your interactions more soul based than transaction based.

## Chapter 16

# TRAITS OF THE GREATS

SPONSORS EXIST IN EVERY SPORT, but not at the level they do in NASCAR. In our sport, in fact, the sponsor *is* the team. FedEx, M&M'S, Bass Pro Shops, Stanley Tools—all become the identity of our team.

Denny Hamlin drives the FedEx Toyota Camry. The brand is the actual identity of our team. As highly involved as FedEx is in other sports, there will never be an NFL team called the Tennessee FedExes.

To illustrate the significance, let's stay with the FedEx example. They have won NASCAR's biggest race, the Daytona 500, three times. The first came in a photo finish, by six inches. The lead story on SportsCenter that day was the race's finish. A company cannot purchase the first few minutes of airtime on SportsCenter as a sponsor, but the same effect is achieved if the company's colors and logo are the identity of the team that wins the Daytona 500. Same goes for the front page of *USA Today*.

Racetrack grandstands are littered with the colors not only of fans' favorite drivers but also of the brands they drive for. The direct connection between driver and sponsor sets a NASCAR sponsorship apart from a billboard or a stadium sign.

When our sponsors show up to a race, they refer to their car as "their team." It is.

When Denny took the checkered flag at Daytona for the first time, I was standing with a large group of FedEx senior executives. They were crying as we walked to Victory Lane. My guess is that they don't cry at other events they sponsor. But their experience was different with NASCAR because their team won. I find so much joy in winning because of what it means to our partners.

In no other sport does sponsor revenue make up as high a percentage of a team's overall revenue as in NASCAR. As a result, sponsors receive a huge amount of relational time and attention from senior leadership of the teams they sponsor. We are the largest item on the marketing budget report of many of our sponsors. We must deliver ROI on their objectives, or we're done.

NASCAR sponsorship no longer is an emotional or ego buy for brands. Sponsorships must be rooted in tangible, measurable results, or sponsors will choose to take their dollars elsewhere.

Through such relationships, I have been fortunate to deal with C-level executives of successful corporations throughout my career. I value seeing behind the curtain of these amazing companies, and I am able to learn from among the greatest leaders and marketing minds in the world. Working with our sponsors is like being enrolled in the best graduate program with my own personal executive coaches. In the process, I have gained valuable insight into what makes their companies so strong.

We take pride in the long-standing relationships we hold with our sponsors. Our average sponsor has been with us ten years, which is a number practically unheard of in sports sponsorships. The few exceptions to that average did not result from sponsorships not working for our partners. Those sponsorships ended because of a change, like a new CEO coming in and wanting to make his or her mark on the company by moving in a different marketing direction. There are more instances, however, of JGR being so ingrained into our sponsors' cultures that even when new CEOs come aboard, they keep our relationship going.

> Long-term business relationships don't just happen—
> they require intentionality.

Each of our sponsors has a secret sauce that we are intimately involved in, and we know exactly where they stand at any moment. The stakes in sponsorships are high. Wins matter. But the reason sponsors stay with us as long as they do is our relationships.

Again, business is relationships.

More than providing a benefit to our partners, our relationships with our sponsors make us better. What I've observed from them has made me a better leader and JGR a better company.

Here is what I have observed about what makes our Mount Rushmore of partners leaders in their respective fields.

## FedEx: People, Service, Profit

FedEx is the most strategic company I have worked with. Just as Joe Gibbs Racing is guided by a simple mission of going fast, FedEx's leaders go to bed and wake up focused on one thing: "PSP," or people, service, profit.

PSP has guided every decision at FedEx since it was founded by Fred Smith in 1971.

FedEx's philosophy is to surround itself with great people, invest in them, and grow them. Those people will then provide outstanding service, which will lead to profit to reinvest back into the business. The folks FedEx hires are second to none.

Over the years, I have had the privilege to learn from Mr. Smith, Mike Glenn (who now is on our advisory board), Raj Subramaniam, Alan Graf, Patrick Fitzgerald, Rob Carter, Monica Skipper, and Katherine Flee. Every time I meet someone in the corporate office and ask how long they have been at FedEx, I usually say, "Wait, let me guess—more than twenty years." Unless the person is too young to give that answer, that is almost always the case, because FedEx invests in its employees.

FedEx employees tend to not want to leave because they have grown within the company, feel valued, and are part of a vibrant corporate culture. Each of them will talk about how difficult decision after difficult decision has been guided by adhering to the people, service, profit mentality. That guiding principle gave birth to what is known as the Purple Promise: "I will make every FedEx experience outstanding." And that is whether they are engaging with a partner, a customer, or a fellow team member. (Sounds a lot like being a fountain!)

Mike and Rob helped put into place the idea that employees will choose to come to work every day with a mindset of contributing to the positive FedEx spirit. They will check where they are on the "mood elevator," assessing what their mood is and adjusting as needed to prepare for the day. Everyone is a vital link. Everyone is accountable for their own well-being. Each employee plays a role in maintaining the FedEx spirit.

What a great lesson for any career—and life, for that matter. All of us could benefit from living the Purple Promise! Make every experience and every interaction outstanding. Breathe life into every transaction. Ask yourself, *Where is my mood today, and what is my role in bringing positive spirit and attitude?*

Mr. Smith is widely known for his optimism. He has never seen a difficult situation that he could not flip into optimism about the future or a growth opportunity. He talks about how wonderful things are when circumstances suggest the opposite. He is the toughest when things are great. Like Coach, he will find an area of vulnerability when things are going great to prevent complacency.

When a new sponsor joins the JGR family, we recommend they talk to FedEx. Regardless of the reason the new sponsor entered the sport, FedEx is the gold standard on maximizing ROI, whether it be through TV commercials or hospitality. FedEx receives more than a billion brand impressions each year from sponsoring Denny Hamlin's number 11 car.

FedEx is passionate about sports and strategic in its use of the platform. Its executives understand how sports can not only enable them to reach new customers but also expand relationships with existing customers.

I have long admired FedEx's charitable work with St. Jude Children's Research Hospital. On a personal level, I will always be grateful to FedEx for their support during our company's most difficult experience. After J.D. passed away, FedEx paid for a full-page advertisement in *USA Today* that paid tribute to J.D.

To me, the JGR-FedEx partnership has been one of the greatest in all of sports.

## Interstate Batteries: A Constant Fountain

In the grand scheme of primary sponsors, Interstate Batteries—our first sponsor—is a small company. We have partners whose marketing budget equals the total revenue of Interstate Batteries. But nobody is more nimble or gets more bang for their buck than Interstate.

Interstate handles everything in-house, with no agencies involved, when it comes to NASCAR. Though a small company, whether it's branding, track activation, licensing approvals, or anything else NASCAR-related, Interstate executes with the professionalism and efficiency of a Fortune 50 company employing a world-class agency.

Coach and Norm Miller, Interstate's chairman of the board, have become best friends whose families vacation together. Norm is a marketing genius, and Coach is so enamored with Norm's ideas and Interstate's manner of conducting business that Coach seems to always be using Interstate as an example for how we should do everything. Remember the "Marcia, Marcia, Marcia!" line from *The Brady Bunch*? The joke in our office is "Interstate, Interstate, Interstate!" Not that we disagree with Coach, because nobody gets more value for what it spends than Interstate.

Interstate was a primary sponsor for fifteen years until the price of NASCAR sponsorships escalated to where it made more sense for Interstate to scale back from sponsoring every race. Their company-wide ability to get more from less is evident in how they market their NASCAR involvement. They are now the primary sponsor for six to eight races a year with the all-green car, which is one of my favorite schemes. Interstate strategically chooses to sponsor races that are spread throughout the season and in the most beneficial locations for their company. Interstate maintains a visible presence at tracks, even bringing customers to races for which they are not a primary sponsor.

They also are a part of the JGR "family of drivers" through smaller sponsorships on all our cars, and they market each team as their own. When Martin Truex Jr. or Denny Hamlin wins a race, they are part of Victory Lane and celebrate even though the car isn't green. It's their team.

To the average fan, Interstate's longevity in the sport combined with its strategic breadth across all our teams produces a much higher perceived volume of their sponsorship.

In our early days, before car graphics were computerized, Norm was meticulous about how his company was branded on our car. When the time came to design his car in the off-season, he flew into Charlotte to be part of the process. We provided him with the blank template of a car, and he pulled out different colored rolls of duct tape, hand cut pieces of tape, and applied them to the car exactly where he wanted them. The designs featured jagged lines, so he had a lot of cutting and placing to do. When Norm finished, he would say, "Take a picture of this. This is how I want the car to look."

And that's how we painted his car. He is the first and only CEO to do that in our shop. That's why we love Norm.

Norm's meticulousness is still reflected in Interstate's attention to detail now with his son Scott running the company.

Interstate's culture carries similarities to ours in that they treat people as souls, not transactions. Their culture is all about building people up— their employees are fountains. The level of care they display is not only for me or Coach or our executive team; they have integrated themselves into the JGR family.

When I see someone at a track in the Interstate bright green shirts, I feel a sense of comfort and peace. It's as though seeing Interstate representatives puts me in my happy place. I always make an effort to talk with anyone I see from Interstate because they truly feel like family.

Personally, I appreciate how the believers at Interstate are not ashamed of its founder's faith. Norm routinely takes part in ministry outreaches and projects, often alongside Coach. The Interstate executives who are Christians are open about their faith, but their company remains inclusive. Being a person of faith is not required to work there, but it's clear that faith plays a role in the company's direction.

Not surprising, Interstate is charitable and takes good care of its employees.

Interstate has been the number one car battery company in the world for two decades, and I believe God has been faithful to the company because of its commitment to sharing the gospel around the world.

Interstate Batteries has been with JGR since the start, and our association is a perfect model of how a partnership should look. I can't imagine business or life without Interstate. I hope they feel the same about us.

## Mars: A Humble Family

In many ways, Mars reminds me of us—a *much* larger version of us. Mars is a privately held family business started by a visionary leader who created a culture and stayed on mission. We have been blessed to work with the Mars company and the Mars family since 2008.

Like Joe Gibbs Racing, Mars follows a set of principles that drives every decision. "The Five Principles," as Mars calls them, are centered on five key words: quality, responsibility, mutuality, efficiency, and freedom:

» We are committed to Quality of work and contributions to society.
» We embrace our Responsibility (as individuals and a company) to act now.
» We base decisions on Mutuality of benefit to our stakeholders.
» We harness the power of Efficiency to use our resources to maximum effect.

» We have the financial Freedom to make our own decisions, unrestricted by motivations of others.

I have heard the words quality, responsibility, mutuality, efficiency, and freedom used a hundred times during our relationship. Those five core principles are Mars's North Star, and Mars stays on mission with those principles.

When Mars went international, they had to figure out how to make a Snickers in Russia taste like a Snickers here. They insisted it be done perfectly.

Making a poor decision about quality keeps its leadership up at night. If a manager cuts corners like, heaven forbid, buying cheaper-quality cocoa, that would be an absolute nonstarter.

As Mars grew, before the company made any acquisitions—and this is a company that recently bought Wrigley—they asked, "Will this dilute the culture?" Any deal had to maintain the company's culture and be consistent with The Five Principles.

From the beginning, the Mars family has embraced our race team as family. I know they are involved in many things, but I take pride in the fact that NASCAR seems to serve as a bond that brings the Mars family together, like a hometown team.

On any given race day, our pits have a Mars family member in them. The Mars sisters often stay in a motor coach inside the track and cook wonderful meals for our team.

The Marses are humble, unassuming, wonderful folks who happen to be part of the biggest and best candy company in the world. You'd never know by the way they act that their company has more than $35 billion in annual sales. Mars's founders did not make themselves bigger than their business. They wanted everything to go back into the company.

Our partnership works so well because we have such similar cultures. And our relationship has led to taking trips to the White House together, planning championship parties, and our being welcomed to the annual family day at Mars headquarters.

**Toyota: No Best, Only Better**

Ask someone at Toyota if their company is the best, and they'll reply, "There is no best, only better."

The Toyota Way consists of two pillars that drive everything the company does.

The first is the relentless pursuit of getting better and is based on the Japanese word *kaizen*, or "continuous improvement," as individuals and as a company. This improvement comes through lots of little steps and constantly asking, "Am I a little ahead of where I was yesterday?"

To call something or someone "the best" would mean comparing to someone else, and comparison can lead to complacency. Those others can't be controlled, the Toyota philosophy goes, but "better" can be.

Toyota's focus is on continuously improving, regardless of what others are doing. For more than a decade, I have observed ever-improving vehicles and ever-improving people at Toyota. Year after year, the Camry is the number-one-selling car in America, but Toyota keeps making it better.

The second pillar is respect for people. Toyota's overarching belief is that people are its most valuable asset and that each person is a valuable part of the team both for what they contribute and who they are as a person.

During our association with Toyota, I have observed a corporate emphasis on teamwork, from Bob Carter on down. Racing is so ingrained in Toyota's culture because it enhances the team feel for everyone at Toyota. Racing also offers a weekly measuring stick on whether the company is continually improving.

Toyota is all about its people and its partners winning together, winning equally, and always getting better.

Jack Hollis, group vice president and general manager of the Toyota Division at Toyota Motor North America, is a business role model for me. He compares *kaizen* to both faith and athletics in his own life. He has told me that neither are areas of our lives where we ever "arrive." Instead, we strive to get a little better each day. He has also told me, "There are only two things that you control: your attitude and your effort. And the only person who knows if you are giving 100 percent is you."

Jack is all about balance. "If you want to be a great president of Joe Gibbs Racing," he once told me, "be a great dad. You have to give 100 percent at both."

Toyota exemplifies a great challenge we all can accept every day. Based on Toyota's pillars, I can ask myself, *Am I giving 100 percent effort at (fill in the blank), or am I just skating by?* And, *Because I control my attitude today, what am I choosing? Am I choosing to be a fountain or a drain?*

Toyota goes as hard as any company I have been around, always at maximum effort. But they also understand the importance of balance and the relentless pursuit of improvement in every area of life.

## TOPICS FOR REFLECTION

1. What would it look like for you to make FedEx's Purple Promise? In other words, what can you do to "make every experience outstanding"?

2. One of the things I admire about Interstate Batteries' people is that every interaction with them fills my tank. Who are the fountains in your organization, and what traits make them that way? How can you be a fountain to those around you?

3. Consider the five key words of Mars's culture: quality, responsibility, mutuality, efficiency, and freedom. Which of these traits do you think your organization excels in? In which do you think there is room to grow?

4. Toyota's belief that there is "no best, only better" helps to guard them against complacency. What are specific areas you can push to be better in your daily work? Your life?

PRINCIPLE 5

# WIN AT LIFE

## Chapter 17

# ACHIEVING THAT ELUSIVE WORK-LIFE BALANCE

WE SEEM TO HAVE ADOPTED a skewed view in our society that bases our perceived value on how much we work. "Cheating on work" is my phrase for doing what is necessary to achieve a work-life balance.

How many of us have had a dinner or a date or games with the kids hijacked by a work-related phone call or text? Work cheats on our personal lives all the time. The most valuable commodity we possess, by far, is time. We try to budget our time based on our life priorities.

If our job cheats on the most valuable thing in our life, shouldn't we find opportunities to cheat on work in the name of work-life balance? And by *cheat*, I don't mean being dishonest or immoral. "Cheating on work" is my dramatic way of describing the small steps we should take to achieve balance.

When an employee leaves the office at four o'clock to take her daughter to practice, she might feel like she needs to sneak out to avoid being considered a slacker. Yet where are the perceived critics that night when she is making phone calls from home or answering emails at ten o'clock?

The business world seems to follow this secret scoring system based on how many hours we work or how many days we spend on the road. Conversations often revolve around our status in this game. Rarely do I hear someone brag that they left the office early for a kid's dance recital. Why not?

Not all occupations are conducive to cheating on work, and some phases of our careers can prevent work-life balance from looking exactly the way we want. Running a small business with no margin or having a job that keeps us on the road can prevent the work-life balance we seek. I doubt many medical students have a healthy work-life balance during that season of life. But later they can. That's fine. Cheating on work can come in small ways.

Those many years I lamented not being fully utilized or challenged, I think God was protecting me and allowing me to have better balance while my sons were younger. As president, my schedule has far less margin now, but my boys are grown, and I am able to find balance in other ways.

Encouraging employees to maintain a proper work-life balance helps Joe Gibbs Racing go fast. If we are winning races but our employees aren't winning in their lives, then going fast will mean nothing. All the trophies we win will feel hollow. Employees who are happy at their jobs, who feel fulfilled by their work, who exercise, who maintain healthy social lives, and who spend quality time with their inner circle are better employees.

Having work-life balance doesn't mean not going hard. Toyota and FedEx employees go as hard as any I've worked with, but those companies also encourage their people to maintain work-life balance.

In all my years of being associated with Toyota and FedEx, I have never heard one of their employees complain about their company. We have enjoyed long associations with both companies, and I have built relationships with employees from various levels on the org charts. If Toyota and FedEx were driving their employees hard through grinding, fourteen-hour days and not giving a flip about their families or personal well-being, I would hear the complaints over a dinner or a casual talk in the garage. Instead, I hear about companies that balance hard work and high expectations with a culture of caring for their employees. In return, the employees are loyal and tend to stay for long tenures. My hope is that JGR employees speak the same way of us.

Work hard, play hard. That's what I want *from* our employees, and that's what I desire *for* our employees.

As president, it needs to start with me. Before I became president, finding balance looked different than it does now, and it was difficult. While my sons were growing up, I missed plenty of games and tournaments because of travel. I had dinners interrupted. I needed to take phone calls while our family was watching a movie together.

Some of us signed up for jobs that make work-life balance more difficult to achieve. Many jobs in NASCAR require being away from home from Thursday to Sunday thirty-six times a year. That doesn't set us up for a great work-life balance during the season. The challenge is finding that balance even if the scale isn't exactly fifty-fifty.

## Setting the Example

Setting the tone with work-life balance is the area where I most miss J.D. in leading our office environment. Now, it is vital to our employees, our partners, and my family that I follow the example J.D. set.

J.D. and I made a pact to hold each other accountable for maintaining work-life balance as we progressed through each stage of parenting. As part of that deal, we covered for each other when possible. One of those areas involved coaching.

We have seven boys between us, and we both made a decision when they were young to be as involved as possible in coaching their sports teams. Our answer to the question of how to coach our kids while running a professional sports organization was this: coach your kid's team and then figure it out from there. If J.D. had an important meeting that conflicted with one of his son's practices or games, I attended the meeting in his place. He did the same for me. I hope how we covered for each other modeled to others in our office that while our business demanded much of our time, was stressful, and involved a lot of travel, it still was possible to have some balance in life through intentionality.

> Companies that encourage work-life balance are better companies because balanced employees are better employees.

J.D. and I took our deal with each other seriously. I coached thirty of my sons' baseball, soccer, and football teams. I was a great coach of kids when it involved snacks, a lot of rah-rah, and just a little strategy or coaching knowledge. Once my boys reached middle school, I was out. My last season as coach was alongside J.D., leading a sixth-grade football team that included my son Collin and J.D.'s son Miller. We went undefeated, and then I pulled a John Elway by walking away with a championship.

There's nothing like coaching a team that includes the grandsons of two former NFL coaches who had nearly four hundred victories between them—Coach and Dan Reeves. J.D. and I would leave our offense on the field on fourth down, and Coach would be stalking down the sideline, instructing us to punt. "They're eleven," we'd say. "We're going to run the ball." (Ever watched a team of eleven-year-olds successfully punt a football? Yeah, me neither.)

J.D.'s commitment to our pact was never more evident than during a crisis-level meeting that ran into the time frame for his sons' flag football practice. We were dealing with a driver-related issue that had started circulating in the media. We had planned a meeting with the driver for the next day, and we were developing a game plan for how to work with the driver and practice damage control with our sponsors. It was the type of meeting during which most everyone gets worked up.

Joe is a fiery coach to begin with, and he grew animated talking about the issue. Our PR person was in the room helping us strategize, and we all had frustrations that complicated the planning. My stomach turned over as the discussion heated up. Ever the levelheaded one, J.D. sat quietly and observed for most of the meeting. Then he broke his silence.

"We'll just sit down and talk with them tomorrow," he said. "This is all common sense, and we're making it way too complicated. He shouldn't have done that, and we'll talk with him tomorrow and make sure it never happens again. You guys can keep talking about it. I'll be back."

J.D. stood, picked up his papers, and started toward the door.

"You're leaving?" I asked.

"Yeah," he said, "The boys have practice."

J.D. headed to practice, and Coach picked up where he had left off in the discussion.

Inside, I laughed, because if there was one thing that would irritate J.D., it was being pulled away from what he considered important because of something he didn't consider more important. I knew his sons' flag football practice was more important to J.D. than this meeting.

Our meeting lasted another hour, and Coach never questioned why J.D. left. If our meeting had required J.D. to stay, he would have done so. But we had elevated a meeting to 9-1-1 level that J.D. didn't believe needed to be a 9-1-1 for him. J.D. knew there would be time for him to plan for the next day.

J.D. always exhibited an ability to discern the true seriousness of situations. He was disciplined, loyal, hardworking, and always on time. He went to all the races. On a number of occasions when someone was in the hospital or a sponsor needed an immediate call, J.D. made a hospital visit or a phone call his biggest priority. He did whatever needed to be done, even when it fell outside of what would be expected of his role as president. But he didn't allow matters to consume his life that didn't need to. When J.D. could, *he* determined what needed to be most important for him, not someone else.

And that afternoon, the remainder of our meeting wasn't more important than his sons' practice.

Inevitably, someone in an office will take advantage of an office environment that promotes work-life balance. What starts as work-life balance with leaving for a daughter's dance recital near the end of the business day turns into taking an afternoon off to take care of an aunt's next-door neighbor's pet. But people who are bought in to the culture, passionate about the mission, and are butt-busters generally do not abuse the system. J.D. used to say, "As long as you are doing a great job at work, do the things you love, make them a priority, and don't apologize for it."

When my boys were little, I followed a system for putting together my calendar. I analyzed any event that involved being gone overnight or going to an evening function that prevented me from being home when the kids went to bed. I determined whether each event was a "have to go" or a "could go." In my job, I *could* go to a work dinner every night for charity functions and industry events. In each stage of my career, I balanced the value of those events and the relational time there against what was going on at home. Invariably, there would be "have to go" work events on the same night as important family events, and I had to make plenty of sacrifices. Many careers require some level of sacrifice. But for every withdrawal I made from my family, I tried to make at least one deposit somewhere else with them.

Having a job that involved traveling to races allowed me to bring the family with me several times a year. By far my favorite races are the ones my family attends with me. I can't imagine going to Daytona, Charlotte, or the season finale without my family. Their opportunities to experience Victory Lane have been the source of many highlights for me.

Balancing work and life is not easy, and I have often failed. But I am grateful for the many memorable moments with my family that resulted because I made spending time with them a priority.

## Work Is Our What, Not Our Who

J.D. knew how to balance work and life because he had unlocked the secret to maintaining a proper perspective about his identity. He never allowed work to consume him to the point that it became the most important thing in his life. His job did not define him.

In all my years with J.D.—from high school through running a major sports organization—separating his career from his identity seemed easy for him. I compare that characteristic to people who are generous with their money. Their perspective comes from seeing themselves as stewards of what God has blessed them with. Money is not an idol to them. Like money, work can become an idol to us. Generous people do not allow that to happen with money, and J.D. displayed the same characteristic when it came to work-life balance.

Our culture is focused on careers and titles. When we meet someone for the first time, whether at a work function, a party, church, or a school program, the first step we often take to identify that person is to ask, "What do you do?" I have yet to hear a person respond to that question with "I'm a great dad" or "I'm a child of God."

We assign so much importance to titles, but titles will not matter on our tombstones. If there are no titles on tombstones, why do we care so much about titles now? It's no wonder work-life balance can become so off. The balance gets thrown out of whack when we allow our entire identity to come from our jobs.

> It is difficult but essential not to allow what you do to become who you are.

J.D. was our company's compass in work-life balance because his identity wasn't wrapped up in being our president. He knew there was more in his life that mattered besides being great at his occupation. Work hard, play hard. J.D. lived that out in front of everyone in our office.

When the president of the company modeled that principle, it was easier for everyone else to follow. But we lost J.D. Now I feel responsible for maintaining that part of our culture. My sons are grown, and without kids at home with practices and games to go to, my personal needs have changed related to work-life balance. Still, I miss the cover that J.D. provided us.

I sense an urgency to not only communicate but also demonstrate for our employees that we value work-life balance. The demonstration is more important than the communication. I need to provide a picture of what work-life balance looks like. Now that my sons are in college or have moved away from home, I find myself looking for opportunities to cover for people who are in earlier stages in their parenting.

I know from experience that kids are young for a short while. I don't want our employees regretting that they've missed a kid's activity. But there also are times when I'm saying, "I'm sorry, but I've got to have you for this. There are times where I'll be throwing you out the door to make sure you're at your daughter's recital. But right now, I need you here." Because of this, I don't mind anyone taking a personal call at work, or printing out the lineup for their son's baseball team on an office printer, or taking two hours for lunch to attend a child's play at school. I promise, we'll get the time back from them at some point!

With our managers recently, we have focused on enabling their direct reports to mention balance in life. If our company preaches God first, family second, and work third, we need to demonstrate that in the way we do business. We must establish processes that provide clear steps to live out that message. And, by the way, that doesn't mean we can't still win half of the races in a season too, because God-family-work doesn't require compromising our team's success. That order actually leads to success.

I constantly wrestle against feeling guilty when I am not in the office or am on vacation, because I don't want our employees thinking I don't care about the company. I struggle to find that balance without J.D. here setting the tone as he always did.

In business—like the rest of us were doing in that meeting J.D. left—we often sacrifice what is important right now for what can be taken care of tomorrow. We overthink. We overprepare. And we miss the practice or the game or the family dinner. To use the deposits and withdrawals analogy again, we keep making withdrawals without making deposits, and one day we find that we have nothing in our account to fall back on.

The fix is not easy. Friends in other industries share about battling the same struggle. Work cheating on life is an enemy, especially with the twenty-four-hour access we have to each other through technology.

J.D. used to talk all the time about how it is hard to be the best at what you do without sacrificing something else. He watched his dad become one of the greatest football coaches ever, but it required Coach to sleep at his office and miss much of J.D.'s and Coy's childhoods. J.D. wanted to be great in his career but not at that cost.

Probably the biggest struggle I face is wanting to be viewed as a butt-buster at work *and* at home. How do we go above and beyond at both, like my friend Jack from Toyota challenged me to do? It's difficult.

The first step in winning the work-life balance battle is surrounding ourselves with like-minded people, holding each other accountable, and covering for each other when possible. It's easier to believe the God-family-work priority structure when you're spending time with other people who believe it too.

Next, determine what is okay to sacrifice. Perhaps it's accepting that we won't be able to pick our kids up from school every day. Or instead of working out five days a week, we work out three. But we also need to determine nonnegotiables and plan as much as possible for what it will take to honor those. Because we can't pick up our children from school every day, maybe we need to give ourselves permission to be a little late to the office a couple of days per week so we can have breakfast with them and take them to school. If you don't have kids, or if you are an empty nester like me, maybe work-life balance involves hobbies, exercise, or an outside passion to pursue. Or being more present with your friends despite your busy job. Aim for small victories. And talk to your employer about your desire.

> The only way to achieve work-life balance is to be fiercely intentional with your schedule.

A great model in being intentional is my twin boys, Evan and Austin. I will attempt to refrain from a massive dad brag, but they are rock stars. Top of their class in high school and college, they are maximizers to the nth degree. Type-A, efficient, always "on," with packed résumés, they make me seem like an introvert. In group projects, they always chose to work with each other because they rarely found others who could go at their pace.

After college, they entered the busy world of consulting, and both are based here in Charlotte. They are in a stage, and a career choice, where work-life balance typically doesn't look balanced yet. But they exemplify being intentional and making the most of their situations. They volunteer by mentoring high school students as Young Life leaders, which includes leading a Monday-evening meeting. It's common for them to work nights. Early on at their jobs, they asked their employers about carving out time on Monday nights. They have a small window for the meetings, but they usually are able to attend and then often go back to work until the wee hours of the night.

Evan and Austin have resolved that their Monday-night meetings bring life to them as well as to those they lead. They also lead a weekly Bible study at 6 a.m. Doing anything at that time of day at their age requires being intentional. They are the same about connecting with friends by calling, texting, and squeezing in get-togethers. They will hop in the car and just show up for their friends. They are the most intentional young adults I have been around. They actually can be exhausting to try to keep up with because they accomplish so much in a day. They even listen to podcasts and sermons at double speed just to be more efficient! But none of the balance they do have would be possible without being deliberate and uncompromising. I am so proud of them, and I take a little pride in the possibility that they got their passion for going hard after what's important from their dad.

Work-life balance is difficult to achieve, and it can look different for different people, different careers, and different stages, but it is possible with intentionality. It requires effort and energy, but what's important is worth pursuing.

Work wants to take. The people in your life need you to give. Honor both.

## TOPICS FOR REFLECTION

1. It is easy for us to let our work define who we are. Think of the things and the people that give meaning to your life. How would your life look different if you put more of a priority on those people and things?

2. I've argued in this chapter that balanced employees are better employees. How balanced is your work and life in this season? Maintaining balance requires intentionality. In what ways can you be more intentional about the balance between work and life? Whom can you enlist to keep you accountable or to help you in this?

## Chapter 18

# INVESTING MOST IN WHO MATTERS MOST

PICTURE OUR RELATIONSHIPS AS CIRCLES. In the outer ring are our acquaintances, our casual relationships—the largest group. The next ring is our coworkers and clients, whom we spend a good deal of time with. These relationships are important to invest in. Then come our friends, some of whom might also be coworkers. These are the folks we often wish we spent more time with. Within that circle is a smaller circle of close friends. Then comes the smallest and most sacred circle of all relationships, our family.

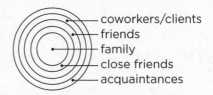

Our work-life balance gets out of whack when we spend a disproportionate amount of our time and energy on the circles farthest from the center. My family and my close friends are the two circles I try to prioritize.

221

My circle of close friends is my "Band of Brothers" group—ten guys, all from high school, who had a life-changing faith experience through the ministry of Young Life. I have no biological brothers, but God gave me these guys instead.

Most people don't keep up with more than one or two friends from high school thirty years later. But our group is special. Each has become a high achiever in life. More important, all have remained faithful to each other even when distance keeps us apart.

For me, winning in life has included finding people who fill my tank and make me better, and then being intentional about pursuing those people even when busyness and geography get in the way. Sometimes that looks like daily banter in our text chain. Other days, it's a Zoom call where we pray for each other. But often it means showing up. We plan "fellas" trips as frequently as our schedules allow. We talk about topics men don't talk about enough when they are together, like how to be better husbands, dads, and employees and how to use our spheres of influence for good. I can think of birthdays, sporting events, and even NASCAR races where several members of the group just showed up.

> Winning at life means investing most
> in those people who are closest to us.

Moose Valliere, who along with J.D. has shared the title of my best friend since college, has demonstrated year after year the importance of being present and showing up.

In 2006, I experienced a mysterious medical scare that led me to schedule an appointment at Mayo Clinic in Jacksonville, Florida. Moose found out about my appointment the night before I was to leave. He knew I wouldn't allow him to come with me if he asked, so he didn't ask. He drove to my house from northern Virginia, and when I opened the door and asked what he was doing, he said, "I'm driving you to Jacksonville. We're going on a road trip!"

I don't remember anything from my appointment, other than that all the test results came back negative. But I do remember eating out with Moose, laughing a lot, watching an NFL game, and smelling some horrible odors in my car. That's what best friends do for each other.

Winning in life includes showing up for the ones you love, even when it is not convenient, and my best friends have modeled that for me.

## Love at First Sight

My immediate, closest circle is Stacey and our sons, Evan, Austin, and Collin. They are my world.

In the summer of 1988, I was standing behind the skateboard counter at my job at Sunshine House, a surf shop in northern Virginia. A stunningly beautiful girl walked in with her family. I immediately headed her way and approached one of the young guys with her, praying he was her brother.

"Hi, I'm Dave," I said. "So . . . is that your sister or your girlfriend?"

"I'm John," he replied. "Yeah, that's my older sister."

"Oh, really. Where does she go to school?"

"She'll be a freshman at George Mason starting in two weeks."

*She goes to my school!*

I introduced myself to Stacey.

"Hi, I'm Dave. I hear you're going to Mason. I'm a sophomore, if you need someone to show you around."

Stacey and I chatted for a few minutes, and she left me with "Hopefully I'll see you on campus." This was before cell phones, so there was no potential for exchanging digits.

When the semester began, my first class was sociology in a large auditorium. I walked in, scanned the open seats, and spotted Stacey. I plopped down beside her and said, "Hey, remember me?"

After class, we sat on a bench in the quad and talked for over an hour. I couldn't believe she was talking to me at all. I invited her to a fraternity party at my house and, to my amazement, she came. That night, September 9, 1988, is what we consider day one of our thirty-plus-year relationship. We sat outside under a tree away from the commotion inside and talked about life, faith, and music. Heck, we could have talked about the phone book for all I cared. Stacey was so special that I immediately thought she personified my dreams of what my wife would be like.

At eighteen, Stacey was wise, confident, and deeply rooted in her faith. Forget that we listened to the same alternative music, loved the surfing culture, and laughed at each other's jokes. Stacey and I shared a chemistry.

Her faith background was much stronger than mine, and in many ways this was intimidating to me, although in a good way, because every time we were together, she made me want to be better. I was Stacey's first boyfriend, and even after twenty-five years of marriage, I often tell her, "I can't believe Stacey Jean Wojciech picked me."

Stacey and I dated throughout college, but it was unconventional. She lived at home until her senior year, and her dad was strict. We were allowed one official date per month. Stacey was the oldest daughter in a family of six kids, and her dad wanted to set boundaries. We were forced to be creative with our time when we were both on campus.

With no cell phones, no emails, and Stacey having a home phone with no call waiting *and* five siblings, communicating when we weren't together presented challenges. I made dozens of stealthy, late-night deliveries of handwritten love letters to her house. I would leave fraternity functions or Young Life events with my buddies to write Stacey a note, drive to her neighborhood, park at the end of her street, and sneak through people's backyards to get to her house. I would place the letter in a Ziploc bag in case it rained, and then I'd tape the bag to her window or hide it under the doormat. Couples nowadays are cheated out of having to pursue each other. How romantic is texting an emoji?

Stacey's father wound up becoming a spiritual mentor to me. He was strict, but he loved and protected his kids fiercely, which I deeply respected, even as a hormone-filled teenager. He managed to communicate his love for me despite the stringent restrictions he placed on us. After Stacey and I had dated five years, I asked him for Stacey's hand in marriage. He hugged me and replied, "You've earned it."

I proposed on Stacey's twenty-third birthday in front of the Washington Monument, on a bridge at the reflecting pool where we had sat on our first official date. The day was a culmination of taking her to all the special spots from our dating relationship, all to the backdrop of a cassette mixtape I had made as our dating soundtrack. Stacey and I married in the summer of 1994.

We planned to wait a few years before having kids, but God had a different plan. Before we headed to the Daytona 500 in 1996, we received one of the best surprises of our lives. During a routine doctor visit, Stacey was given a pregnancy test followed by the news that we would become parents. During the first ultrasound, I turned on my video camera, zoomed in on the nurse, and said, "We don't want to know what we're having."

She looked directly into the camera and asked, "Do you want to know how many there are?"

"We are *not* having twins," Stacey responded.

"Oh, yes, you are," the nurse said.

At twenty-seven years old, the T-shirt guy became the father of twin boys, Evan and Austin. Three years later, Collin completed our family.

Those early years seemed so difficult, with changing lots of diapers and trying to make a name for myself at work on little sleep.

Being a dad has been my greatest joy in life. Parents don't have the benefit of practice or a playbook. We make it up as we go along. From the day we brought the twins home, I resolved that I wanted no regrets when the boys were grown. I would be as all-in as I possibly could, because I knew the season of life when my boys were small would be short. But I had no idea how quickly that season would pass.

I had a saying: "Enjoy your kids, don't endure them." Having small kids and a career is plain hard. Sometimes it isn't fun. But on this side of that stage, I've learned that we tend to long to experience those days again. The best advice I can give someone still in that stage is to enjoy each minute. Of all the difficult things I have done in my life and my career, the three most difficult were sending each son off to college. The night before the twins left for college, I wrote in my journal,

It's actually happening. The day I've dreaded for almost 19 years. It's the first time I've ever been upset getting ready for a family trip. Normally, that's my happy place—loading the car for another Alpern adventure. Only this trip is different. There won't be an amusement park or a beach, there won't be singing in the car or fighting over who gets to pick the movie. There won't be a vote on where we go to dinner or who gets what bed. And after this trip, only three of our family of five get to come home. Tomorrow we take our twin baby boys to college.

I have been counting the days down in my prayer journal for a year. I felt sick to my stomach when the number got to double digits (99), and last week I just stared in disbelief at the page after I wrote the number 9. Today the number is 1. One more night in their bed. One more time I will walk by their room and touch the door and pray for them as they are tucked away in their beds asleep. One more day to trip over their shoes by the side door. I don't know whether to stay up all night and make it last or to curl up in a ball and cry myself to sleep. . . .

When Stacey was pregnant with the twins, she gave me the verse, Psalm 127:4-5 "Like arrows in the hands of a warrior are children born in one's youth. Blessed is the man whose quiver is full of them." It's my favorite verse. My problem is I covet that quiver full, and I am having a tough time accepting that eventually those arrows get shot out into the world. "Eventually" is tomorrow.

I know I'm supposed to be the strong one; I'm the dad. Yet, here I am, a guy who got through giving my own father's eulogy without so much as a sniffle, weeping at the sight of my son putting his clothes in a bin. It just can't be. How many nights have I sat in this room, laughing, crying, praying with these boys? Just yesterday I told him how great he did in his T-ball game; it was last week that I told him how proud of him I was for doing so good in his Christmas pageant. Didn't we just go trick-or-treating? Was this all just a dream? A crazy, wonderful, storybook dream?

It's a cruel fate, this parenting thing. Our lives are turned upside down when kids arrive, chaos becomes the norm, then, in the blink of an eye, they grow up. And then they leave for college. Roughly 6,900 days we get 'em. 6,900 dinners, 6,900 goodnights. 6,900 days to model to them what a godly life looks like. I have used up 6,899 of them. I can't fathom that I only have one left. . . .

I know tomorrow will be a mix of emotions, and I will probably lose it many times, but as I drive home I will set my mind on one thing: Thanking my Lord for the privilege and honor he bestowed on me and Stacey in entrusting us with the most amazing, wonderful, brilliant, hilarious, special boys on the face of the earth. What a joy it has been, and will be, to do life together. . . .

I love you boys.

For the record, the college thing turned out great. If ever there were people created to be college students, it was my twins. And Collin, too, has thrived at Belmont University. We love visiting him in Nashville, and we love being college parents.

Having our boys at home was a gift I never wanted to end, and now I face a new, very different stage of life as an empty nester.

If I write another book, the topic will probably be fatherhood. In my years as a dad, I learned to enjoy my kids and not beat myself up when I screwed up. Comparison is the thief of joy, and it's the parents who fall for the comparison trap. Think about it: I am the only dad my boys have ever had! I learned to not worry about how other dads were doing this or that. Parenting is about being the best parents *we* can be.

I thank God continuously for my wife. I know beyond the shadow of a doubt that I could not have done my job alone. Stacey has offered me wise counsel and fervent prayer, and she has been the voice of reason in my career time and time again. Stacey, by far the most glamorous woman I've ever seen, chose an unglamorous lifestyle of staying home with our boys and poured the spiritual foundation of their lives. She embodies grace and wisdom, and she lives out her faith in the way she handles everything in her life. She has a hunger to learn Scripture and to study the works of heroes of the faith like J. R. R. Tolkien, C. S. Lewis, and Dietrich Bonhoeffer. There are many things in life I am not sure of; I have unanswered questions and plenty of insecurity. But one thing I know for sure is that I married the right person.

Life often makes more sense in hindsight. George Mason was not my first choice for college. To say my freshman year was awful would be an understatement. I packed my Volkswagen Rabbit myself and lived off campus with guys not even in school in an apartment I found through a newspaper ad. All my friends had gone off to college away from home, and I was lost and uninterested in my engineering classes. I felt like a complete failure. I wept many nights in my tiny bedroom, questioning why God was punishing me, trying to figure out what I had done wrong.

In hindsight, I see God's faithfulness to me. He directed me to a school where I was close to my mentor, Rick Beckwith, so I could do ministry with him during college. He knew that my best buddy, Moose, would transfer there, as would another member of our Band of Brothers,

Gumby. And most of all, God knew that George Mason was where I would fall in love with the girl of my dreams, my soul mate, Stacey.

I often compare life to a book. A page, or perhaps even an entire chapter, might not make sense. If we could flip ahead and see what happens in the following chapter, life would be much easier. When we do get a few chapters ahead, we understand more what had happened previously. It's that "Oh, now I get it" feeling.

The good news is that God wrote the book. He knows how the story ends. I have tried to live in a way that I trust him for the next chapter while embracing the one I am living—even when my tendency is to want to change the script or skip ahead.

But twenty years into my career at Joe Gibbs Racing, I found myself entering another chapter of life that didn't make sense.

## TOPICS FOR REFLECTION

1. Part of winning at life is keeping our priorities straight, investing most in those who matter the most to us. Look at the circle diagram on page 217. Think about who in your life fits into each circle. Now look at how you spend your time and effort. Are there any changes you need to make going forward?

2. Who are the people who made it possible to reach where you are now? Make a list of the things they did to support you. How can you express your gratitude to them now?

## Chapter 19

# NOT THE SAME OL' J.D.

Starting in late 2012 and into 2013, something was different about JGR's compass. About *my* compass.

Although the differences were subtle, something seemed wrong with J.D. He smiled less and appeared distracted at times. I chalked up the changes to a midlife crisis.

J.D. might have been the most spiritually aware person I have met. The idea expressed in Hebrews 13:14—that this world is not our home, that "we are looking for the city that is to come" in eternity—J.D. got that.

Growing up with J.D., I never saw anything that seemed to bother him, because he walked around with a big-picture perspective on life. Nothing negative stuck to him; he dealt with it and moved on. Even having money didn't seem to affect J.D.

But then J.D. began talking more about contracts and people disappointing him. When we added a car and hired more people, contracts and personnel issues bothered all of us. They seemed to get to J.D.

more than the rest of us, and more than I had ever seen anything annoy him. Our company was continuing to grow, and work was becoming increasingly stressful for us. I thought J.D.'s job was finally starting to wear on him.

J.D. seemed distracted more frequently. I would talk to him, and he would not pay attention or would stare at his phone or computer. Then I would follow up the next day, and J.D. would act like the conversation had never happened. "Dude," I would say, "we just talked about this yesterday." But J.D. couldn't make the connection.

In spring 2014, Todd and I sat down with J.D. and encouraged him to take a break, possibly even a six-month sabbatical to recharge. We assured him that we could cover for him while he was out.

"Nah, I'm fine," he replied.

That summer, Stacey, the boys, and I headed off for our annual beach trip with friends from high school and their families. On the way, J.D. called and asked what he should do when he arrived at the resort's gate. "Um, tell them your name and they'll let you in, like always," I said. Thirty minutes later, J.D. called and said, "Hey, I'm about an hour away. What do I do when I get to the gate?" I told him again. He called a third time with the same question.

During that week, J.D. didn't pay attention during conversations. He would suddenly fall asleep. When we reminisced about stories from high school—which had always excited J.D.—he stared blankly. He wasn't the same ol' J.D.

The guys on the trip assumed work stress was causing J.D. to check out, and they confronted him and said he should consider stepping down from his job. When they mentioned J.D.'s condition to me, I confided that he had been acting that way for over a year. But that trip was the worst I had seen him.

The following month, JGR held a news conference to announce our signing of Carl Edwards to drive our new, fourth car; the addition of Arris as a sponsor; and our partnership with Carlos Slim. I was the emcee, and J.D. sat on the stage as our president. J.D. usually owned those types of events. He was funny. He was quick-witted. He flashed that J.D. smile that communicated so much so simply. J.D. was the person we wanted up front when the camera lights came on. Yet that day, he bombed.

He read everything verbatim from his note card, with no emotion or eye contact. His speech was slow and slurred. After the event, my phone blew up with people asking if J.D. was on medication or if something was wrong with him.

Something was terribly wrong with J.D.

I called Melissa, his wife. Melissa and I have known each other since fifth grade. After she and J.D. married, our families vacationed together. She and my wife are best friends. So are our sons. Melissa is like a sister I can have any conversation with.

Before I could start to express my concerns, she told me, "Dave, I already know what you're going to say."

Two weeks later, Melissa secretly took J.D. to Mayo Clinic for a brain scan. He didn't return with a diagnosis. The best way I can remember the results of the scan, very much in layman's terms, was that "he had some stuff going on in his brain."

J.D. never received a precise diagnosis, but he had frontotemporal dementia—a general term for a group of brain disorders of the brain's frontal and temporal lobes, which help control a person's personality, language, and behavior. After J.D.'s death, his brain was sent to Stanford University for study.

Because J.D.'s illness was rare and somewhat mysterious, we had no idea what his life expectancy was. We had no road map for how the disease would progress.

Their sons knew something was wrong with their dad, but J.D. and Melissa didn't want them to know specifics for as long as possible. Melissa requested that we not make J.D.'s condition public, because she wanted to keep life for the boys normal for as long as she could. Only a handful of us even knew of J.D.'s trip to Mayo Clinic. Once the media found out, normal would become impossible to maintain.

When I was finally able to tell my sons about J.D.'s disease, one of them said, "Dad, I thought everything worked for good for those who love the Lord. You said J.D.'s your most faithful friend. Then why did this happen to him? It's not fair."

I agreed. "Guys, you're right, it isn't fair," I said. "I can tell you that."

Their questions were ones I had been asking myself. I had no answers for them.

What I did know, though, was that God loves us. And during my experiences in college that didn't make sense at the time and through the other valleys in my life, God had always remained faithful. God's definition of good is different from ours. I tried to assure my sons that through the pain and confusion and all the uncertainties regarding J.D., we needed to trust God so that his good would result from J.D.'s illness.

Per Melissa's request, we kept J.D.'s condition private, even within the company.

Coworkers would come into my office and ask, "What's wrong with J.D.? Why is he acting like this?" I couldn't answer them.

As much as I could, I attended NASCAR meetings at which J.D. normally represented our team. But there were many meetings that J.D. still went to himself, insisting that he continue to lead the company. He probably should not have attended most of those meetings. In NASCAR circles, J.D.'s appearances fueled speculation that he was on medication, or worse. I wanted to protect my best friend. I wanted to prevent him from being so vulnerable, but I didn't know how I could.

At the start of 2015, the disease's effects on J.D. were becoming more evident, and we had to wrestle with a choice: Do we deal with the consequences of making J.D.'s illness public or the consequences of not saying anything and having a team president embarrassing himself and exposing his family to awkward questions and speculation? Which option was better for the family? Which protected J.D. more?

We waited a painstaking six months after J.D.'s Mayo Clinic visit before going public. In late March, we called a team meeting. J.D. spoke for himself, standing and saying, "I know that God has a plan. God puts us through things for a reason."

Midweek before the race in Martinsville, Virginia, we released a statement to the media stating that J.D. was undergoing treatment for "symptoms impacting areas of brain function." That Sunday, a few hours before the Cup race, Coach addressed the media for the first time in person, calling J.D. "my hero" and offering few answers about his son's condition and prognosis—because we lacked real answers.

At the time, J.D. was still capable of being involved in the company's day-to-day operations at the office. But he needed help, and those of us who were aware of his condition did our best to cover for him.

Behind the scenes, I took part in gut-wrenching conversations.

Because J.D. had a degenerative neurological disorder, his disease's progression included deterioration of muscular components somewhat akin to amyotrophic lateral sclerosis, or Lou Gehrig's disease. Melissa was pragmatic about J.D.'s illness. With four sons and J.D. to care for, she needed to be. Coach, on the other hand, had difficulty acknowledging that the disease was advancing. Coach wanted J.D. at as many meetings as J.D. wanted to attend and to continue to handle as many of his normal responsibilities as J.D. wanted to. As a dad, my heart understood Coach fighting against the signs, because, as J.D.'s best friend, I agreed with him. But I had to think about what was best for J.D. and Joe Gibbs Racing.

In one of the most heartbreaking conversations I've ever had, I went to Coach and told him that J.D. shouldn't drive anymore.

"He's going to kill somebody," I said.

"J.D.'s driving is fine," Coach countered.

"It's *not* fine," I said. "What if he hits somebody or causes a big crash?"

Coach and I had several heated conversations, even screaming at each other at times. I got it—J.D. was his son. Coach had started this race team to share with J.D. and Coy. I couldn't imagine how devastating it had to be for Coach to see both J.D. and his dream slipping away. I would have fought, too, if it had been one of my sons, and every time I went into Coach's office for one of those difficult conversations, I tried to put myself in his shoes. I tried to process through the heart of a dad.

More than getting into it with each other over J.D.'s condition, Coach and I had many tender, heart-to-heart talks. Before J.D. became sick, I had never seen Coach cry. While J.D. was sick, it's not a stretch to say that Coach and I cried with each other dozens of times.

Able to acknowledge what Coach could not yet, I believed that when J.D. couldn't act like the company president, I needed to, even without the title. I needed to insert myself into discussions that I knew J.D. would have been in—even if no one asked me to insert myself. I knew J.D. so well because I had been beside him through every chapter of JGR's history. I could handle things the way I believed J.D would if he were healthy.

I knew what I should do. I just didn't have the self-confidence to take that step.

Every month seemed to lead the effects of the disease into a new stage, and each stage grew worse. With little medical insight in terms of a firm diagnosis, we had no clue what would come next. The physical and mental debilitation progressed in uneven proportions. J.D. could no longer put his shoes on. He struggled to walk. He lost his ability to talk.

J.D. came to the office every day for the first few years of his disease, being driven in, when that became necessary, by Mike Lepp and Brad Fiehler and an amazing team of people who cared for him. But every day when I came to work, I had to see my best friend deteriorate. Every time I said to myself, *It can't get worse than this*, it did. And that cruel cycle continued for four years.

## Unwanted Promotion

Bob Dyar, our chaplain, entered my office and closed the door.

"I had this strong urge to tell you that you need to be the company president," he began. "We need somebody, and you're the only one who can do it. It might be a long time before they officially make that happen—it's inevitable. But in the meantime, you should start acting like it."

It was like the Lord was prodding me.

*Yes, I know I should do this. And now the* chaplain *is confirming it.*

I reluctantly started following Bob's advice. At least six more people came into my office at different times to tell me something to the effect of "I think you probably ought to take J.D.'s title for now, because we publicly need someone in that role. People know J.D. is sick, and they are asking what we're going to do."

We were reaching a point where we needed to take some kind of step forward. Drivers had told us for several years that one of our company's distinctive appeals was that with Coach in charge and J.D. the president in his forties, JGR had a clear succession plan. Now, all we had were awkward questions.

In September 2015, I was part of a meeting that included Coach, J.D., and Todd. Todd spoke up.

"I think Pern needs to be the president."

I knew how Todd felt because of our close relationship. But I had no idea Todd would say that to Coach—and in front of J.D.

"Well," J.D. asked, "then what do I do?"

"You're an owner, and you can continue to do the things you're doing," Todd said. "But Dave can go to a lot of meetings."

Todd explained why he thought the transition was best for JGR. J.D. was okay with Todd's proposal, although it looked like something didn't sound right about the idea to him—like the conversation confirmed that something really was wrong with him. Still, J.D. might have liked the idea more than I did. I understood why Todd made that pitch, and I appreciated his heart and courage in doing so, but I wasn't ready to accept the ramifications of someone else—especially me—taking on J.D.'s role.

Throughout my career, and even after being promoted to chief marketing officer a couple of years earlier, I had desired more authority and more respect. Now, here I was on the verge of becoming the recognized acting president, but under circumstances that made me not want the role. If J.D. had come to me and said, "I'm going to take on a role as owner, and we're going to name you president," I would have been excited about the opportunity. But assuming additional responsibilities because my best friend was sick offered no appeal. All I wanted was J.D. healthy and in the office full-time, cutting up, making people laugh. Even knocking ice cream cones out of my hands.

For years, I had been like a copilot, and as long as J.D. was holding the controls, I felt comfortable. But with J.D. able to hold the controls less and less, I felt uneasy. Like I was unprepared. Add in the unforgiving march of J.D.'s disease and seeing my best friend's time in the office gradually reduced to coming in solely for rehab with our trainers, and I felt inadequate to handle not only the business side of Joe Gibbs Racing but also my emotions.

I was losing my compass.

When we won the Cup championship in 2015, Coach and I flew on the team plane to the champions dinner. I spent most of the trip imagining Coach thinking, *This is supposed to be my son with me.* Coach had built this company—his family business—to one day hand over to J.D. Now here I was, taking his son's place. Coach did not make me feel that way; that was my own insecurity. But the future certainly wasn't supposed to unfold this way.

As the start of the 2016 season neared, I had been attending NASCAR competition meetings on behalf of JGR, I had filled the president's role for the '15 postseason awards ceremony, and I had attended the NASCAR champions dinner with Coach, a role reserved for the owner and president. It was such a surreal time. Everyone treated me like the president even though, technically, I wasn't. If I acted like I wanted the role, I would feel like I was betraying my best friend. If I ran from the role, that would feel equally dishonorable to Coach and his family business that needed someone in that position.

Coach understandably remained hesitant to make the move permanent. We prayed regularly for J.D. in our meetings. We believed that God could heal him. In our eyes, officially removing J.D. from the president's job would have been an acknowledgment that our prayers wouldn't be answered the way we wanted. That J.D. would not get better.

On February 4, 2016, I became president of Joe Gibbs Racing.

I have only patches of memories from the meeting where that move became official. I remember I was sitting in Coach's office, at the same table where I've sat thousands of times. I sat in the same spot in which I had laughed almost uncontrollably at Coach's football stories, had knock-down drag-outs over business decisions, and helped recruit Dale Earnhardt Jr.

But I don't recall how Coach told me about the change. Looking back, that meeting seems like an out-of-body experience. Here is the one thing I most remember: in some ways, it was the worst day of my life. My first thought wasn't of the work I needed to get started on or how quickly I needed to get up to speed to handle the competition side of the company. In that moment, my career did not matter. I had just been named president of Coach's family business when the sole goal had been to hand the company over to J.D.

Sitting across the table from Coach, I realized, *This is final. J.D.'s not getting better.*

We held a team meeting to announce several changes to the executive team. We issued a press release with all the transitions, including J.D. becoming a cochairman with Coach, me filling his president's role, Todd resigning as COO to pursue other options outside the company, and Coy coming on board to work on the operations side in addition to running the JGR motocross team he had started in 2008.

From the beginning, J.D., Todd, and I had been together. Todd had shared for some time that while he had the perfect job for him (and it was), he had felt God calling him to step aside for something else—perhaps something he could start himself using his incredible organizational skills. Todd didn't know what was next; he just felt it was time to leave. He remained with us as a consultant for a period of time before he moved to Montana. I miss Todd every day.

J.D., Todd, and I had complemented each other perfectly, and in every scenario we dreamed up, we assumed a much longer run together as JGR's three musketeers. Somebody, somewhere, had ripped our script to shreds. If there were Vegas odds on which of us would be the last one standing at Joe Gibbs Racing, the odds of it being me would have been a million to one.

As I was accepting congratulations and responding to texts from friends who had heard the news, I couldn't help but think, *This sucks. I was just given J.D.'s job. I don't want this. I want J.D. to be healed.*

Near the end of a long, emotional day, I was at home trying to process all that had taken place over the previous twelve hours. My cell phone rang. It was Kyle Busch. Normally when a driver calls at night, it's not to chat about a ball game but because there's a problem. On this night, I thought perhaps he was calling to congratulate me. No such luck. He was angry about an issue with a sponsor and wanted me to fix it.

I tell about that call not because I was frustrated with Kyle; the reason for his call goes back to his singular focus on our mission, which makes him a great driver. Calls like that are part of dealing with elite athletes who want to win—which is why when I hung up, I muttered to myself, "Darn you, J.D. That was supposed to be your butt-chewing, not mine. Thanks for dropping this in my lap." Those were the types of calls J.D. handled so well, and at that moment the gravity of me now being the recipient of these calls struck me.

In my journal that night, my account of the job change was short: "Well, I'm the president of Joe Gibbs Racing. I wish I was still the T-shirt guy. Lord, sustain me."

NOT THE SAME OL' J.D.

The rest of the page was filled with concerns about my family and struggles my sons were going through at the time. My burden for my sons was greater than my professional uneasiness. I believe that if J.D. could have read my journal entry, he would have told me, "That a boy, Pern. Way to have your priorities straight!"

Two weeks later, we were in Daytona to start the new season. As we did every year, my family arrived early and stayed in the same house we always rented, although at that stage of their lives, our sons couldn't stay the whole time. I took the "Look how much we've grown" photos with my boys as I did every year. But so much else was different.

One day, alone in the house, I wrote in my journal,

Kind of surreal. I'm at this house for the twentieth straight year. The first time, I was the T-shirt guy. Didn't make much money, nary a care in the world. Todd, me, and J.D. just having a ball. Now they're both gone. My family is off doing life and I'm here alone, the president of a 500-plus-employee sports empire. And I hate it. Lord, sustain me, and infuse my life with joy, health, and enthusiasm. Give me strength and wisdom. I'm going to need it.

Looking back on that entry, I am surprised I used the word *hate*. I didn't hate my new job. But that word choice shows the depth of my emotions coming out of a grueling year and a half of keeping J.D.'s condition secret, being unable to refute the speculation surrounding him, trying to protect my best friend, and dealing with the uncomfortable period as "acting" president—both discreetly and publicly. With Todd leaving and who knew what we could expect with J.D.'s condition, I prayed the whole thing wouldn't implode.

The day of the 500, J.D. showed up at the track. He was making races occasionally at that point, and I guess no one should have been surprised to see him show up for our biggest race. His presence made for a perfect day.

When the white flag came out to signify the final lap, Denny Hamlin was in fourth place. But he made a great run and in Turn 4, he was side by side with future teammate Martin Truex Jr. for the lead. They stayed right next to each other, making contact a couple of times, all the way to the finish line. Denny nosed out Martin by 0.010 seconds—the closest finish in Daytona 500 history.

That day marked our first trip back to Victory Lane at the Daytona 500 since 1993. It came with a driver that J.D. had signed to a development deal with our team. It came in the number 11 car that bore J.D.'s football number. And it came on J.D.'s forty-seventh birthday.

All circumstances considered, it was a victory that our entire company desperately needed.

## TOPICS FOR REFLECTION

1. How do you make sense of difficult times that don't go according to plan? Where do you turn for strength or guidance?

2. Todd had the guts to speak up during a difficult emotional time for the good of the company. How are you with speaking up during a tough situation? What gives you courage in times like these?

## Chapter 20

# CARRYING ON J.D.'S LEGACY

BEFORE J.D. BECAME SICK, even in the times when I lamented what I perceived to be a lack of respect for my contributions to the company, I never envied J.D. for his position. I often told him, "I can't imagine what it would be like to go to bed at night having all these employees on your mind." J.D. would just chuckle.

Now, I carry the burden of going fast and bringing in money. Along with that comes the responsibility of looking out for the employees who help JGR fulfill our mission. The answers to all my questions have to be found in the same way that J.D., Todd, and I had found them since the start of the company: through a lot of prayer and a lot of "just figure it out."

No one handed me a Joe Gibbs Racing manual for how to do the president's job, and neither of the other two musketeers—my brothers—is here.

I can no longer walk around the corner and into J.D.'s office and ask, "Hey, what would you do about this?" In the past, whenever a crisis came up, we went into a meeting room with whichever leadership team was appropriate for handling the crisis in order to solve the problem. Regardless of the circumstances, if J.D. was in that room, I knew everything was going to be okay. Now, without him, my thoughts are, *Well, I think everything is going to be okay. I think this is how we approach this.*

The Friday-night double dates with our wives have ended. When our family is staying at the beach house we shared with J.D.'s family, I catch myself thinking, *If J.D. were here, we'd be going for a run right about now.* But he's not there. And I'll never go for a run with him again.

I invested a lot of time in my friendship with J.D. We raised our families together. I am big on traditions, and our families shared many traditions I consider sacred, like ski trips, beach vacations in South Carolina, and going to Disney World and Universal Studios every year at the start of Daytona week. I am committed to continuing those traditions with J.D.'s family.

Throughout every stage of life, J.D. was my picture of what a Christian dad looked like. What a Christian business leader looked like. When he passed, I felt like I was almost having to start over in so many facets of life. J.D.'s death left a huge emptiness that will never be filled.

Through the lens of faith, I know that I don't have to like what has happened. I trust in God's sovereignty. I trust in his promise that everything works for the good of those who love him.[5] I accept that God's definition of good is different from mine. The good he has for J.D. is that J.D. is in paradise now, no longer suffering. The next time I see J.D., he'll walk and talk and smile like the healthy J.D. I choose to remember.

I find comfort in the knowledge that there are many people still alive whom J.D. led to the Lord during his too-short time with us. And I feel a sense of responsibility to pick up J.D.'s mantle.

When J.D. passed, God already had a plan prepared for me, and that helps me accept that I'll be okay without J.D. I have an amazing group of friends. Many of us share a link with J.D. through our Young Life group from high school. But most don't live in Charlotte. Moose and Gumby came down from our hometown in northern Virginia frequently for all four years of J.D.'s illness to visit him and his boys. That's what brothers do. But I miss that too. I can see them every month or two, and I can call or text whenever I want. But that's different, because J.D. was such a significant part of my day-to-day routine.

This isn't what I signed up for. J.D. was taken from me, and now I have his job. I signed up to work with J.D., not to *be* J.D.

J.D., Todd, and I were like three legs of a stool with each of us looking at issues from our different angles and balancing the weight of the company. Coach knew that if J.D., Todd, and I were in agreement on a decision, we had talked it out and sometimes even had it out with each other to reach our agreement. Generally, if the three of us agreed, Coach knew our decision was the correct one. Two-thirds of those complementary pieces are gone, and I don't have J.D. and Todd to run ideas past, to balance the weight of a decision. It's difficult to be a stool with only one leg. I don't have their perspectives to consider. Neither does Coach.

What's really missing is J.D.'s steady, measured voice of reason. His commitment to make the morally correct choice and his courage to make decisions that always favored people. His determination to exceed expectations by doing what's right.

That's why my guiding question as I lead Joe Gibbs Racing is *How would J.D. handle this?* When I make a decision that might not make sense from a business standpoint, the managers who were here with J.D. know where that comes from.

I better than anyone grasped the importance company-wide of J.D.'s ability to never take himself too seriously. Even in the tensest times, J.D. emitted a tone of lightheartedness with that same smile that earned him "Sunniest Smile" in our high school senior yearbook. J.D. is the only person I can make this claim about: since meeting him in the seventh grade, I never heard him complain about one thing. Ever.

J.D. set the tone for our entire office. He also possessed the ability to make people feel valued. J.D. was super at remembering people's names and knowing one or two things about them. He would take a moment to ask someone how they were doing as their paths crossed in the office. The interactions were quick, but they were long enough for that person to know that J.D. remembered them and had been thinking about them. That he cared about them.

Even as J.D.'s illness progressed, the disease never rattled him. Up until his death, J.D. carried an inner confidence in God and his destiny, and nothing—not even a cruel, unpredictable disease—could shake his faith.

Personally, J.D. always made me feel like I was the only person he was dealing with. I never heard him say, "You have no idea how much I have going on. I've gotta go." Whether in one of our offices or in the hallway—outside of work, even—when J.D. and I talked, I felt like my topic was all he was thinking about. In a stressful environment like ours, that's difficult to do. But J.D. did it all the time. Since taking on his role, I am even more amazed he could do that, because now I have a sense of how much he actually was dealing with.

Before becoming president, I knew the blueprint for a lot of the rooms of the house, but I didn't have the entire blueprint. As chief marketing officer, 95 percent of my job was outside the building. I knew the industry and the sponsors, but I possessed limited knowledge of the inner workings of what went on inside our own building. The team planes? All I needed to know about them was when to board! But once the entire blueprint for JGR was rolled out across my desk, I acquired a whole new level of respect for J.D. and the job he performed so well.

## Preparing for the Next Season

Honestly, even to this day, I'm not totally comfortable being the president of JGR.

J.D. died on January 11, 2019. When Kyle Busch won the Cup Series championship that season, I had been president for close to four years. Stacey and I flew with Coach to NASCAR's postseason awards banquet in Nashville.

Later that night, Stacey told me, "This didn't feel right. It felt like it was supposed to be J.D. and Melissa with Joe."

I replied, "I was thinking the same thing."

I'm a planner, and I never would have planned for this. Joe Gibbs Racing is a family business, and my last name is not Gibbs. But perhaps, just perhaps, J.D. was preparing me for this job. For certain, I believe that during those seasons when I was tired of being the T-shirt guy or the PR guy, when I was feeling that I had been made for more than what I was doing, God was preparing me for a job I never imagined I would fill.

As much as I have questioned "Why me?" as president of the Gibbs family business, I also have asked, "Who else but me could carry on J.D.'s legacy?"

I have made a career of not being the best at anything. I'm not the best at math, and I'm not the smartest businessperson. I cannot list many things at which I consider myself great. I have to surround myself with people who are better than me at my deficiencies. But mixed in with all my insecurities is the realization that I am the one unique link to J.D.

His fingerprints are on everything here. If we want J.D. to live on in JGR's culture, it needs to start with me because I was the closest person to him other than Coach and Coy.

I am grateful Coy also answered the call and came over from running our motocross team when Todd left and J.D. got sick. Coy handles the competition side now and is a co-owner with his dad. Coy is nothing like J.D., yet exactly like J.D. He has a much tougher exterior than J.D. had but just as soft a heart. I know God also has been preparing him for this, and in many ways it is probably equally tough for him.

Since I knew J.D. so well, I pretty much know on what side he would land in any decision. In meetings now, that responsibility energizes me. It motivates me. Even when I am unsure what to do, I think about how J.D. would handle the situation.

We have many people in our company who didn't work with J.D. when he was fully healthy. They didn't know what J.D. was truly like. That number keeps growing, and each year that passes, our company moves further from how things were when J.D. led us. Sometimes that becomes a burden for me as I seek to keep his fingerprints visible.

For example, J.D. treated this company as a ministry. I recognize that I have not been as intentional about that as J.D. was, but I am trying to approach each day asking the question, *How is this my ministry?* When I receive a text from an employee or a partner that is not the response I desired, I have learned to not take the text personally by remembering that this company is my ministry and that the person on the other end of that text is my ministry. I am not in this position to argue and bellyache; I am here to reflect the God I serve in a way that draws others to him. J.D.'s standard that I compare myself against is extraordinarily high, and God definitely is growing me in this area. There remains plenty of work to do.

J.D.'s example of maintaining the highest priority on winning in life is one I need to follow. To properly lead this company, I need to have a healthy marriage and be a good dad. I need to take care of myself physically, emotionally, and spiritually. I need balance in my life, and I must understand that only when I do all those things am I then in a position to add true value to this company.

As much as I doubt my abilities sometimes, I recognize that I wouldn't be here if I was not called to be here. I don't know how many years this season of my life and career will last, but it is my season to carry on J.D.'s legacy. I owe so much to the Gibbs family, and I am motivated to fill this position by my loyalty to them. For now, the Gibbs family needs me to serve their company as president, and I will do so as faithfully and competently as possible for as long as my season lasts. For as long as I can continue to add value. Until God directs me elsewhere.

But, ultimately, this is a Gibbs family business. J.D.'s office remains unchanged from his last day at work. Whenever we meet in Coach's meeting room, we leave J.D.'s seat next to his dad open. No one sits in J.D.'s chair or takes his place.

No one *can* take J.D.'s place.

I'm excited about mentoring J.D. and Melissa's sons—Jackson, Miller, Jason, and Taylor—as they get started in this business. What a joy it will be to watch them and their cousins, Coy's kids—Ty (who might be driving one of our Cup cars in the not-too-distant future), Case, Elle, and Jett. We will place them in the departments where they fit best, and I'll keep telling them the stories they love to hear about their dad and their Uncle J.D. Of course, when they're working here, I'll knock some ice cream cones and sandwiches out of their hands. J.D. would want it no other way.

I need to be around to show the Gibbs kids how the company works and teach them how J.D. would lead us, because I am the one to do that. And then one day, when it's time for a change in season, I will pass the torch to the next Gibbs to run this company.

Because that's how J.D. would handle this.

# Afterword

IF J.D. KNEW I WAS WRITING A BOOK, he would poke fun at me. "About what?" Then he would add, "Are you going to charge people for the book?" But I know he would then turn serious. "You'd better share your testimony, because that's the most important thing you have to say."

You're right, J.D.

My faith journey was different from J.D.'s, but he was a significant part of my journey.

I grew up feeling like there was some sort of Supreme Being, because the idea that the universe and earth poofed into existence from nothing seemed illogical. As the son of an engineer, I knew from the second law of thermodynamics that order leads to disorder—that we don't just get something from nothing. Yet the idea of a personal God seemed foreign to me.

My dad was Jewish and my mom Protestant, but we did not attend church. In fact, I did not set foot in a church until my senior year of high school. The closest we came to any type of religious activity was celebrating Christmas as a family, although we did not celebrate for religious reasons.

Not until I started attending Young Life meetings at the Gibbs home did I hear the message of the Bible that Rick Beckwith presented: that God created everything, came to earth in human form in Jesus Christ two thousand years ago, lived a perfect life, died on a cross, and was resurrected from the dead so that he could provide salvation for all people through a personal relationship with him. The message sounded like folly, a wild fairy tale. I remember thinking that if I told my dad that I believed what I'd heard at Young Life, he would say I had lost my marbles.

My dad actually approved of my attending Young Life. Even though he disparagingly referred to what I was hearing at the meetings as proselytizing—not to mention "intellectual suicide"—he liked the friends I was hanging out with there and said they made a positive impact on me.

I even attended a small-group Bible study in the home of John Colston, a volunteer leader with Young Life. I wanted what I was hearing to be true, but it seemed too far-fetched to accept as truth.

I read two impactful books my junior year of high school: *Evidence That Demands a Verdict* and *More Than a Carpenter*, both by Josh McDowell. The first book especially resonated with me because it detailed how McDowell, a skeptic like me, set out to disprove Christianity and instead became a Christian.

The determining factor for me as to whether Christianity was legitimate was whether Jesus Christ's resurrection actually occurred. As I had applied an engineer's logic to my questions about Christianity, if Jesus Christ rose from the dead, then all the other questions I had didn't really matter. In other words, if the one thing that seemed most ridiculous could be proved, then the rest could be accepted as true. But if the resurrection account was false, then none of the rest of my questions mattered.

As I read and studied, the evidence supporting Jesus' resurrection both from the Bible and reliable historical documents overwhelmed me. I was particularly struck by the fact that his disciples saw Jesus after he rose from the dead and then most of them were martyred for standing by their claims of his resurrection. You won't find many who will protect a lie or a hoax all the way to their deaths.

But I also had the visible evidence in the lives of people like J.D., Rick, and John that all pointed to a real, personal, loving God.

That "something different" about J.D. that I had noticed began to connect to what I was learning about Christianity. The more I heard and read about the God of the Bible and what a Christian lifestyle should look like, the more I realized that J.D. was putting skin on what it meant to believe in all this. Plus, if J.D. believed what I was hearing, it seemed less hokey to me.

My senior year, a year and a half after attending my first Young Life meeting, while sitting in John's living room at one of our Bible studies, I accepted Jesus Christ as my personal Lord and Savior.

If my story of faith is evidence of anything, it's that you do not have to figure everything out to become a Christian, and becoming a Christian does not mean that you *will* figure everything out. I still have questions I wrestle with. Some are difficult questions that I can't answer. I have also long struggled with doubts to some degree. But I have come to realize that's why we have the word *faith*.

Christian faith is about giving all you know of yourself to all you know of Jesus Christ, no matter how much or little that is. Becoming a Christian is not about being perfect or taking a magical pill that solves all your problems. Instead, it's about living an imperfect life the best you know how by following the playbook written by the one who created you.

Two years before my dad passed away, he made the same decision to give his life to Jesus. Dad had been diagnosed with non-Hodgkin's lymphoma, and he and I were having more spiritual discussions. I had expected that if my dad wound up becoming a Christian, he would do so because of what he read in apologetics books. After all, he was an extremely smart guy who arrived at decisions logically.

Instead, Dad made his decision because of relationships he had with three men who showed they cared about him and modeled the love of Christ for him.

One was with the pastor of a small country Baptist church in Georgia, where my dad moved after retiring. The second was Coach, whom my dad greatly respected and who was the first person to pray with my dad over the phone. The other was my father-in-law. I wouldn't say that my dad and Stacey's dad were especially close friends, because they didn't spend much time together. But they had a special conversation during a dinner meeting. My dad and Stacey's dad were both electrical engineers, but Stacey's dad was more family focused than career focused, and he was the person who, late in my dad's life, was able to teach him what was most important.

Not only did my dad accept Christ, but Stacey and I had the extra-special pleasure of watching my dad and our three sons be baptized together in that little country church.

I think back to Rick Beckwith having the guts to walk into my high school and share his faith with me, regardless of my response to his message. Rick could have discounted me as a skeptic and given up on me, but he kept hanging out with me and investing in my life. I think of how his introduction to the ministry of Young Life and, more specifically, the Christian faith changed who my friends were, impacted who I married, and transformed the entire trajectory of my life. Rick starting a friendship with me and J.D., modeling his faith through his life, eternally altered three generations of my family.

I reflect often on an illustration I learned in high school. Picture a line that is infinitely long to the left and infinitely long to the right. In the middle of that line is a speck that represents our lives. What we do on that speck determines our eternity, and that should give us a sense of urgency to live our lives the right way and to follow the game plan that God has written for us in Scripture.

J.D. and my dad are gone. I miss them both every day. For whatever reason, God has chosen to give me time here beyond what J.D. and my dad had. But because of the decisions they made from their very different circumstances to accept Jesus as Lord and Savior, I take heart in knowing that I will see them again and that we will spend eternity together.

# Acknowledgments

My father started writing his CIA memoir when he got sick. I tried to convince him to record his thoughts in case he wasn't able to finish, but, ever the optimist, he declined. He died three chapters in.

I decided then that while my story may not be an exposé of a spy like his, it was no less important to share my story of God's faithfulness to me and my unique career journey for future generations of my family. So thanks, Dad, for the inspiration to start and finish this book.

My acknowledgments must start with the key characters in my story—my family members, starting with my wife, whom I've loved since she was seventeen. If ever there was the definition of a soul mate, it is my Stacey. Thank you for sharing life with me and for inspiring me to be a better man every day. You are my best friend, and I still can't believe you picked me. To my boys, Evan, Austin, and Collin, it is the greatest joy in my life to be your dad. There's no way to properly describe how proud I am of each one of you, not just for what you do but most importantly for who you are. You are wonderful sons. Just know the best part of my job has been the special moments it has provided the five of us to enjoy together.

To my mom, my sisters, my in-laws, and my many nieces and nephews, I love each of you, and it gives me such joy that my job has allowed many of you to cheer along with me.

To Joe Gibbs for your trust in me and for letting me tag along on the ride of a lifetime. To J.D. for being my role model and the entire Gibbs family for welcoming me and my "Dave's Plans" for all these years.

To Don and Todd Meredith for welcoming me in to JGR and for your unmistakable part in helping to make it what it is today.

To everyone at Joe Gibbs Racing, past and present, thanks for being the secret ingredients that have built our culture and made this company a family for so many.

To all the sponsors, partners, industry executives (some of you are named in this book, but many of you are not)—the relationships with you have been the highlights of my career.

To my band of brothers, the "fellas" from Oakton High School, thanks for giving me a picture every day of what true friendship and character looks like.

To the ministry of Young Life, to my leaders Rick and John, and to all of the staff and volunteers who have the guts to walk into the lives of kids, I'm grateful that you stepped into my life and changed it forever.

To Tyndale House Publishers, specifically Carol Traver, for letting me tell my story! Thanks to Jonathan Schindler, Jillian Schlossberg, and Christina Garrison. You treated this rookie author like a veteran, and I promise if I ever write another book . . . never mind.

To the team at WTA Media: Brian Mitchell—you believed I had a book in me and got all of this started! I appreciate you and also David Schroeder for the encouragement and creativity.

To my cowriter, Dave Thomas, definitely the better Dave at writing! I could not have done this book without you. Thanks for organizing my messy thoughts, stories, and outlines—you arranged the furniture beautifully!

To you, the reader, *thank you*! I hope my story encouraged you in some way.

And to my Creator, God the Father, thank you for loving me and for your free gift of salvation through Jesus.

# Notes

1. "MBTI Basics: Thinking or Feeling," Myers & Briggs Foundation, accessed November 20, 2020, https://www.myersbriggs.org/my-mbti-personality-type /mbti-basics/thinking-or-feeling.htm.
2. See *The Five Love Languages* by Gary Chapman.
3. Tourette Association of America, *TouretteConnect*, September 27, 2019, https://tourette.org/touretteconnect-september/.
4. "FAQs," Tourette Association of America, accessed December 1, 2020, https://tourette.org/about-tourette/overview/faqs/.
5. See Romans 8:28.

# About the Authors

**DAVE ALPERN** began his career with Joe Gibbs Racing in 1993 as an unpaid intern. Since then he has held nearly every position in the front office, including overseeing consumer products, communications, and sponsorships before being named team president.

As one of the longest-tenured executives in the sport, Alpern has seen the team grow from eighteen employees to more than five hundred and has worked with C-level executives for many of the world's top brands, such as Toyota, FedEx, Mars, Stanley, the Coca-Cola Company, and Comcast. Dave has been invited to the White House on multiple occasions after winning NASCAR championships in 2000, 2002, 2005, 2015, and 2019.

Born in Frankfurt, Germany, as the son of a high-ranking CIA official, he returned to the States at age two and grew up just outside the nation's capital in Northern Virginia. He attended Oakton High School (along with childhood friend J.D. Gibbs, the son of Hall of Fame Washington Redskins head coach Joe Gibbs) and earned a degree in communications from George Mason University in Fairfax, Virginia. His plans to pursue an MBA were put on hold in 1993 when he was offered an internship with Coach Gibbs, which led to a move to Charlotte, North Carolina, and a one-company career that is now in its third decade.

Alpern is a regular university guest lecturer, particularly at the

University of North Carolina Kenan-Flagler Business School for both their undergraduate and graduate business programs. He teaches on marketing, sponsorship, and social media, and also enjoys corporate speaking.

Dave is married to his college sweetheart, Stacey, and they have three sons: twins who recently graduated from the University of North Carolina at Chapel Hill and an audio engineering student at Belmont University in Nashville. His interests include snow skiing, snowboarding, surfing, and playing an occasional round of golf. He is also an avid fan of the Washington Football Team, the Washington Capitals, and the North Carolina Tar Heels.

DAVID THOMAS is a sportswriter and author of numerous books, including *I Still Believe*, *Impact Player*, *All In*, and *Remember Why You Play*. A lifelong Texan and graduate of the University of Texas at Arlington, he lives near Dallas, Texas, with his wife and their two children.